The Politics of Micro-Decisi

Digital Cultures Series

Edited by Armin Beverungen, Irina Kaldrack,
Martina Leeker, Sascha Simons, and Florian Sprenger

A book series of the *Digital Cultures Research Lab*

The Politics of Micro-Decisions: Edward Snowden, Net Neutrality, and the Architectures of the Internet

Florian Sprenger

Translated by
Valentine A. Pakis

With a Foreword by
Christopher M. Kelty

μ meson press

**Bibliographical Information of the
German National Library**
The German National Library lists this publication in the
Deutsche Nationalbibliografie (German National Biblio-
graphy); detailed bibliographic information is available
online at http://dnb.d-nb.de.

Published by meson press, Hybrid Publishing Lab,
Centre for Digital Cultures, Leuphana University of Lüneburg
www.meson-press.com

Design concept: Torsten Köchlin, Silke Krieg
Cover Image: © Lily Wittenburg

The print edition of this book is printed by Lightning Source,
Milton Keynes, United Kingdom.

ISBN (Print):   978-3-95796-040-5
ISBN (PDF):   978-3-95796-041-2
ISBN (EPUB): 978-3-95796-042-9
DOI: 10.14619/005

The digital edition of this publication can be downloaded
freely at: www.meson-press.com.

This publication was funded by the "Niedersächsisches
Vorab" program of the Volkswagen Foundation, by the Minis-
try for Science and Culture of Lower Saxony, and the
EU major project Innovation Incubator Lüneburg.

Contents

„Decisions are a stage for many dramas."

– James G. March und Johan P.
Olsen, *Ambiguity and Choice in
Organizations*

45 3c 2a a5 d4 31 40 00 40 fd 47 8b 32 74 05 05 51 13 91 26

Christopher M. Kelty

I am delighted to forward Florian Sprenger's extraordinary packet with this header attached. As Sprenger's piece argues there is no communication without interruption, which I do so here at his request. I forward this packet—with its time-to-live decremented by one—but not without having done some "deep packet inspection" first. I urge the reader to do the same, and to send it on to the next node.

Sprenger's piece is both political and media theory. If you think there is nothing left to say about Paul Baran's famous 1964 work on distributed networks, then Sprenger's reading may surprise you. Indeed, it is only in the wake of Snowden's recent NSA leaks and a decade of fighting for net neutrality that the interrupted message of Baran's invention is finally getting through, and it doesn't say what most people assume that it does.

What Sprenger highlights—possibly for the first time since Baran—is the importance of the "micro-decisions" which route our communications to and from each other in the networks we rely on every day. These decisions necessarily interrupt communication, though at a speed imperceptible to humans, allowing us to tweet and chat and stream and torrent, whether contentedly ignorant or anxiously suspicious of every word. Indeed, in any given instance of communication today there are a mind-boggling number of decisions made at every node in our networks, routing petabytes of data here and there, according to tests and rules and codes whose conception, legislation and implementation are complex, intricate, and sometimes lost to history.

12   Sprenger highlights Baran's invention of a communication system that "flows in bursts"—a coherence in contradiction that enables both the experience of a real-time communication network and the reality of its constant interruption and execution. Baran's article dwells on the necessity of processing messages at each node—a possibility only imaginable in the era of digital computers that can spend their time—like over-caffeinated postal workers—comparing and sorting information about messages and the state of the network all day and night.

I process this packet here at UCLA—down the street from where Baran penned his article at RAND. UCLA likes to bill itself, without any reasonable justification, as "the birthplace of the internet." It is actually "the site of the initiation of the first host-host connection made over the first general-purpose packet switching network, except for the one conducted by BBN staff with teletypes hooked directly to their minicomputers in order to demonstrate the algorithm"[1]—but that's not much of a T-shirt. What UCLA can boast is the first *Interface Message Processor*, or IMP. The IMP is precisely the "micro-decision-maker" at the heart of Sprenger's story; they were minicomputers whose sole function in 1969 was to collect information about the state of the network, make decisions about what to do with a packet, rewrite the header and send it on to the next IMP or Host connected to an IMP. IMPs have long since disappeared—as processing power and memory function increased, the functionality of the IMP was moved inside the operating systems of mini-computers and main-frames and servers, making the standardized set of protocols called "the TCP/IP stack" a ubiquitous feature of now billions of devices. Now we carry our decision-makers with us everywhere, though they are not exactly "in our pocket," so to speak.

---

1   I am indebted to Bradley Fidler of the *Kleinrock Center for Internet History* for this precision on UCLA's role, which is otherwise quite significant, even if it isn't the "birthplace."

One might ask, though, whether there is more than one kind of decision making at stake here? Are these in fact the decisions of a democracy—a rule of law? The "micro-decisions" of our IMPS are not the singular decisions of the sovereign—à la Carl Schmitt—they create "exceptions" only locally, and if they do, it is precisely the goal of the design to route the packets elsewhere, to update the network, and to delegate power to other micro-decision-makers. Which is to say, it is very much a radicalization of the idea of the rule of law; perhaps the most elaborate and extensive system for the rule of law yet imagined. Lawrence Lessig's famous chestnut that "code is law" would seem to be a starting point for Sprenger, and yet even that provocative equation leaves open many questions. For such a "rule of law" involves at least two aspects of decision-making—the *legislative* and the *administrative.*

The micro-decisions of IMPs are most likely to be *administrative*—not the decisive creation of laws, but their execution. Taken together, all these micro-decisions make up a blindingly fast, hyper-efficient, automated, *neutral* bureaucracy. But it is a utopian bureaucracy: *a dream of a bureaucracy without corruption.* Such decision-making is easily and everywhere perverted—so much so that it is a nearly full-employment act for cyber-security researchers around the globe.

The *legislative* decision-making of the Internet is of another kind. It is not the decision-making of machines, but the design decisions of those who conceive, implement, code, update and maintain them. In a democracy, the setting of rules is a *procedural* solution to the problem of politics—one that keeps us, in the best case, from killing each other over our differences. The arbitrary powers of another, or the fanatical differences in the Hobbesian state of nature are supposed to be yoked to the process of deliberation, debate and decision. And yet for the Internet, decisions are arbitrary in the precise sense that no democratic procedure gave rise to them. These legislative "micro-decisions" of the engineers, software architects, protocol designers, the builders and maintainers of the networks and software and backbones and interfaces are largely undemocratic—especially when undertaken by large, opaque global corporations from Nokia and Motorola to Google and Apple to Cisco, Level3, T-Mobile or Sprint—who are, to differing extents, required to execute the wishes of the global security and cyberwarfare elites in government.

Which is also to say, it is a democracy of *epistemè* not *doxa*; not a clash of opinions played out in an election or a public sphere, but the reign of the philosopher-kings of the Internet: engineers, designers, corporate managers, academics, military strategists. Strangely and once upon a time, the Internet was explicitly conceived in opposition to such a republic. The real radicalism of the Internet was not its technical structure (packet-switching, end-to-end, TCP/IP etc), but the open system of revisable engineering standards enshrined in the *Internet Engineering Task Force*—an organization with increasingly little power over the very global network it ushered into existence. The storied IETF system of issuing *Requests for Comments* in the public space of the Internet itself at least aimed at a democracy of *legislative* micro-decision-making, even if its utopic vision could never be compatible with the competitive autocracy of corporate telecommunications and networking companies and their surveillance overlords.

And so this (unconstitutional) *constitutional* moment in the creation of the internet (RFCs, the IETF and the promise of neutrality—all in all a very Rawlsian moment) buckled under the weight of power. It still forms a "mystical foundation of authority" over both technologists and activists (we who continue to support net neutrality and an open Internet free of surveillance), even as it is systematically dismantled from within through the relentless "tyranny of the margin" driving every innovation, every update and every act of maintenance.

And so we have instead—as we always seem to—a representative democracy. But it is a peculiar one, consisting of an unelected expert elite whose most specific desire has been to engineer a system resistant to the power of unelected expert elites. This is what accounts for the dreamlike promise of a *democratizing* Internet, but not necessarily a democratically instituted one. The dream of a democratizing Internet is not just that it will usher in or actualize democracy, but that it will remain perpetually open to the future, always revisable. The hope is that one can always recall a change, periodically revisit a decision, or balance the abuses of today with the possibility of the future. Perhaps.

But there is another side. Imps—of the classical mythical sort—are not decision makers, but tricksters, gremlins, parasites in Michel Serres' terms. They delight in disrupting the communications of humans. This ambivalent figure remains a necessary one when considering the political field of the Internet today. On the one hand, after Snowden, we can harbor no illusions of a network free of control, surveillance, conspiracy and deception. But nor can we have illusions of a perfectly neutral one, a "democratizing one"— this is *a fantasy of revolution without terror.*[2] If our nodes are impish at all, they enable the exploits, attacks, hacks and pranks that permeate and confuse the contemporary network; they introduce unpredictability, confusion, breakdown, neurosis: *indecision.* Perfect control—even for the NSA—would remain out of reach.

But even as the decisions are un- or anti-democratically made, they nonetheless produce the communicative ground for any kind of public dispute, and from this ground emerges the figures of political rationality in the post-Internet era. Neutrality, anonymity, privacy, and conspiracy name aspects of this political rationality—but they are attributed to an Internet we no longer have, an Internet that has been interrupted. It is as if the engineers of that old Internet had sent a message saying "this network is neutral and democratic"—but it was a long time, and many decisions later before the legal scholars, social scientists and media theoreticians received it, even though they

2   I steal this lovely notion from Rosalind Morris.

experienced it as being instantaneous, real-time, immediate—without history even. The network was labeled neutral; our map was updated; time-to-live was decremented; the network promised to democratize; but the message came too late because the message *always* comes too late.

Title IP Header Decoded:
- – Version: 4
- – Header length: 5 (20 bytes)
- – TOS: 0x3c (See page 11, RFC 791—net neutrality never existed)
- – Total Length: 0x2aa5 (10917 bytes—German version will vary)
- – Identification: 0xd431 (arbitrary)
- – Flags and Fragments: 0x4000 (Don't Fragment | 13 bit offset)
- – TTL: 0x40 (64 hops)
- – Protocol: 0xfd (Experimental)
- – Header Checksum: 0x478b
- – Source: 0x32740505 (50.116.5.5[kelty.org])
- – Destination: 0x51139126 (81.19.145.38[floriansprenger.com])

Introduction

Every bit and byte that reaches our devices has already traversed a long journey through invisible infrastructures. Such bits arrive as parts of data packets from the expanses of digital networks and are then processed with other bits into a text, image, or sound. Along their way, every bit packet crosses numerous nodes where, in the short amount of time required by temporary storage and buffers, a series of micro-decisions is made by means of established protocols—a decision about the most efficient path to the destination, a decision about the processing speed, a decision about the priority of incoming packets. These micro-decisions interrupt the stream of data in order to control its distribution. The stream never flows uninterruptedly.

Those decisions are not associated with individual decision-makers; rather, they are effective because they take place automatically—in unfathomable numbers and as quickly as possible—according to a fixed set of rules.[1] They conflate the levels of the social and the technical: Their protocological regime was determined in negotiation processes between various interest groups and they generate connections or disconnections between the people at the end points of the network, but they are technically implemented by means of binding protocols for

1 In his book *Protocol*, Alexander Galloway extensively describes the significance of the Internet's protocol architecture as a mode of exercising power in societies of control: "Protocol is how technological control exists after decentralization" (2004, 8). Building upon this approach, the discussion presented here will focus on the micro-decisions that are enabled by this protocol architecture. Whereas in Galloway's work the mechanisms of power are more or less unspecified and protocols seem to be merely given, here I will address questions concerning the conditions under which power is exercised, where it is exercised, and when. Despite the ten years that have passed since the publication of Galloway's book, his arguments remain as topical as ever. Thus it seems reasonable to extend his ideas to certain discussions that have since been taking place, in particular to the discussions that have been concerned with net neutrality and Edward Snowden's leaks.

the sequence of processes.[2] These strictly determined sequences are carried out in a rigidly automated manner without any regard for the people communicating and the contents of the communication. Political and economic considerations have been made in the background to these micro-decisions, because the technical development of digital networks starts with their implementation. In their multifaceted nature, such micro-decisions have been a highly neglected dimension of control and surveillance in the twenty-first century, while their importance has taken on new shapes in ever emerging digital networks. They represent the smallest unit and the technical precondition of a present-day network politics—and of our potential opposition to it.

Micro-decisions appear at first as an effect of current changes and as a technical manifestation of global exertions of power. On its own, however, this perspective is insufficient. In light of the pervasiveness of global access and the social sphere, forms of digital transmission have made it clear how deeply these micro-decisions are entrenched in the present. This essay is an effort to seek out some of their places and times, for it is primarily their locality and temporality that can provide us with insight about their political dimension. Micro-decisions do not take place in parliaments, political hot spots, or police stations but rather in data-processing centers or server farms at the level of technical infrastructures. They are also at home on our own computers, devices, and gadgets. Their places are the nodes of networks.

The time of micro-decisions is the interruption that stops every transmission at every given node, so that decisions can be made about the direction and priority of its journey ahead. Without these decisions there is no transmission. The fact that transmissions are constantly interrupted not only means that they are

---

2   Laura DeNardis (2014) has provided the most recent discussion of Internet governance, the political significance of establishing protocols and standards, and the difficulties associated with their implementation.

never completed in putative real-time, that people are never connected immediately, and that we have no direct access to the world we are connected to. Interruptions are also the precondition for decisions. Decisions require time. The interruptions free up this time by adding durations of stasis to the temporality of transmissions. These durations occur at places of decision-making whose location can be determined, namely at network nodes that are subject to governmental or economic authority and depend on technological developments. In order to map out the extent of these decisions, it is necessary to know when, where, how, and why transmissions have been interrupted instead of simply dismissing interruptions as temporary setbacks to the success of communication.

All decisions regarding further transmission in one direction or another or in one sequence or another are thus tied to specific preconditions in space and time. That said, they should not be understood as intentional, human acts. Rather, their effectiveness derives precisely from their automation, their sheer number, and their speed, all of which surpass human understanding because of their involvement at every second in the transmission of every bit packet. Micro-decisions have always been made by computers for computers. In terms of the logic of decision-making, the basis of all computers and their networks is not only structured on the level of binary code but also on that of the protocols that produce connections and disconnections, participation and non-participation.

The purpose of this essay is to trace some of the origins of the Internet's architectures—understood as the rules and plans that organize its structure—and the development of its places and times and thus, from a historical perspective, to come closer to understanding some of their underlying technical preconditions and political and economic goals. What will become apparent is that such micro-decisions can reveal much about the state of the political systems in which they are made. Whereas their protocols have been discussed in great detail by the likes of Alexander

Galloway and Eugene Thacker, and a number of studies—by Janet Abbate, Sebastian Gießmann, Mercedes Bunz, for example—have been devoted to the general history of the Internet, the focus here will rest on the role of the decisions themselves. In order to understand our present situation and the current state of digital cultures, we are in urgent need of some insight into the scope of these decisions. It is hoped that such insight might allow us to contest future decisions of this sort before they are made and to identify possible alternatives.

A Civil War on the Internet

As abstract as the preconditions of such decisions might seem at this point, their consequences are quite concrete. In fact, if any faith can be had in the urgent ideas of the theorist Harry Halpin, an "immaterial civil war" is presently being fought over the sovereignty of digital networks (2013). Representatives of the new world stand in opposition to those who wish to transfer the relations of the old, pre-digital world into the new. Micro-decisions are central instruments for exercising a type of sovereign power that is valid in both worlds. Their standards, architectures, and protocols are currently up for grabs. Halpin and many activists tend to believe that the original architecture of the Internet represents a guarantee for its democratic, pacifist, and freedom-securing function and that net neutrality is a fundamental digital right. Nonetheless, the necessity of decisions is already ingrained in this architecture as well, however dem-ocratically it had indeed been conceived. In other words, there can be no Internet without control (though certainly without surveillance) and there can be no transmission without the exertion of power (though certainly without discrimination).[3]

3   Chris Kelty (2014b) has argued that freedom in digital cultures has to be
     implemented in technologies in order to be effective and to oppose their
     neutralization.

All things are equal to the protocol that governs the decisions. Hierarchies and conventions of appropriate behavior are established only after the implementation of the protocol. The protocol's task is to generate this hierarchy. Yet everything about which decisions are made and can thus be transmitted must, according to Galloway, take the form that the protocol has predetermined for the purpose of processing: "Standardisation is the political reactionary tactic that enables radical openness" (2004, 143). The possibility of sending various types of data on the Internet is based on the rigid standards that have been set by protocols for decisions. If something does not possess the predetermined form, it does not appear on the Internet. The content of these forms (that is, of our emails, our telephone calls, and our browser histories), however, is separated from the decision, and today it is a matter of dispute whether that which is transmitted even ought to be decoupled from the process of transmission. Efforts are being made from various sides to know the contents of communication or to make its transmission more profitable.

Some of the front lines of such disputes are taking place under the banner of so-called net neutrality. In light of the leaks released by Edward Snowden, moreover, it is now quite clear to see what is at stake. My thoughts below will operate between the two poles of net neutrality and the surveillance practices of the National Security Agency (NSA), which ought not to be separated from one another but are only seldom united. Both are essentially based on the same media-technical possibilities provided by micro-decisions. In technical and political terms, the places and times are by and large identical at which net neutrality ceases and NSA surveillance begins: in the interruption of transmissions at the nodes of the network. It is therefore all the more important to consider the context of both arguments. They are two sides of a coin that has been imprinted in equal measure by the technologies and architectures of transmission. In many senses, they admittedly point in different directions—they are concerned with different economies, different political intentions, and different legal foundations. From the perspective of media theory as presented here, however, their uses are closely related and their positions in the present are adjacent.

The following discussion will revolve around issues of control taken as the distribution of data that takes place at the nodes and backbones of providers. Thus control, on the one hand, means access to the header in order to examine whether a packet satisfies the protocol's requirements. On the other hand, control means regulating the decisions for routing. Surveillance, on the contrary, I understand to be the attempts to gain access to knowledge about the content of packets or to gain information about the social networks of those who are communicating by means of meta-data analysis and graph-theoretical applications. This distinction between control and surveillance is important because the control of a network can be automated and can thus form a necessary component of network architecture without any surveillance, though the potential for surveillance is necessarily implied. Ultimately, and despite the ever-growing potential of its automation, surveillance can always be traced back to an act of intention, and to that extent it is anything but arbitrary. For there is an entire series of actors who are not only interested in the knowledge generated by such automated surveillance; they are also capable of establishing or undermining the rules of protocols. Providers would like to distinguish time-critical data from data that is less time-critical in order to fulfill demands in a more customer-friendly manner and maintain their commercial network operations. Intelligence services and cyber-criminals live off of this sort of knowledge.

In recent years, intensive debates have taken place about whether providers—which grant Internet access to paying customers and which own and operate the Internet nodes or hubs through which all traffic has to pass—should treat all data packets equally without any intervention or whether they should be allowed to look at data packets before they transport them. These debates, which will be treated in the first part of this essay, have been fueled by a controversial reality: In order to give preferential treatment to one packet or another, the packet's contents must be known. The surveillance of data traffic implies a non-neutral Internet. The opposite is true of control as a form of data management: It is the precondition of data traffic and thus the precondition of neutrality as well. In common Internet protocols, control guarantees that anything can be transmitted at all, and this is because all packets are treated equally. Decisions about the sequence, speed, and reliability of transmissions in this sense are supposed to be neutral, which means that the control over the distribution of packets should disregard their content, volume, users, services, or applications. Such micro-decisions can only be neutral if what is being transmitted is unknown. In an ideal manner, and on account of encryption, this happens to be the case with the Internet protocol TCP/IP because the latter only allows for headers to be read. At the present moment, it is precisely this issue that is being reevaluated by Internet providers and undermined by the NSA and other intelligence services, while agencies such as the US Federal Communications Commission (FCC) are trying to establish legal foundations for sustainable net neutrality. Nonetheless, based on the same technical foundation, the hardware used by all of the actors begins to operate at the same location and at the same time: in the interruption of transmissions for the purpose of making a decision.

Control is based on the meta-data from the header of a packet, which, like a parcel label, has to be legible to every node and contain the sender's address, the address of the destination, and other instructions for processing.[4] In the case of control in the

4   The legal status of such meta-data is largely unclear. Whereas the American government argues that meta-data are not private because their accessibility is necessary simply for sending a message—that is, its sender inevitably allows such data to be read by a third party—a legal decision on this matter has yet to be made. For the moment, the NSA's large-scale collection of meta-data is justified by Section 215 of the Patriot Act, which allows such measures to be taken for the purpose of fighting terrorism even without a court order. For this reason, Barack Obama stressed in his first

sense of network management, these meta-data are typically not stored. With the help of graph-theoretical processes, however, their patterns can be made to reveal a great deal of information about their contents. They indicate interconnections and target criteria. The meta-data gathered from mobile media are far more informative than those of static addresses because they include profiles about a given user's movement.[5] Accordingly, surveillance is not necessarily dependent on viewing content; it can also operate on the basis of the patterns and addresses that are subject to controls. In this way, an act of surveillance can secretly target a transmission that is seemingly neutral and thus undermine this neutrality. Even the traffic monitored by the NSA can be transmitted in a net-neutral manner, but then this neutrality is worth far less than it seems.

The debates held about these questions are the most recent and perhaps the most exciting expression of the demand that the rules for such decisions should not be established in private or secretively (that is, without the participation of those concerned) but should rather be negotiated publicly. In these debates, and quite consequentially, the technical foundations of the Internet and political demands are blended together according to a democratic basis of networking—in other words, it has become clear that Internet politics cannot be managed without technical

public statement about Snowden that the government makes a strong distinction between content and meta-data (see White House 2013). There are signs, however, that the US Supreme Court will argue, after the expiration of the Patriot Act in June 2015, that digital networks have changed the conditions and our understanding of privacy to such a great extent that new guidelines will be necessary for classifying meta-data as private. In that case, the NSA would need court approval to collect the data of any single person (see M. Cohn 2014). In Europe, this decision has already been made: Like IP addresses, meta-data are treated as private according to the EU's privacy and data-protection laws.

5   For instance, whoever uses the Android operating system on his or her smart phone and has connected its location-based services with Google Maps can view the location data that Google has stored at http://maps.google.com/locationhistory/.

knowledge and that technical networks can never be unpolitical. The deliberations therefore view networks not as explanations but rather as something to be explained, following the intuition of Chris Kelty (2014a). In this regard, as Geert Lovink has suggested, the event of Snowden's revelations has brought an end to the age of "new media," washed away the final vestiges of naive cyber euphoria, and underscored with the utmost clarity that the Internet is a political space (2014).

In order to understand what is at stake in all of this, the second half of this essay will adopt a media-archaeological approach and focus on a technical paper by Paul Baran. Published in 1964, "On Distributed Communications Networks" provides the theoretical foundations of what we today call the Internet (1964d). Using the term "packet switching," Baran was the first to formulate the principle of basing a transmission network for digital data, which have been divided into packets, on micro-decisions that are made at every node and no longer simply on data processing at the transmission or receiving stages. His work provides a blueprint for the current debates because it designates the very times and places of decision-making that are still valid today. In light of the changed nature of the challenges that face us, a return to Baran's paper will make it obvious which epistemological preconditions the present technical processes are still obeying, how they have managed to conceal these preconditions, and where their political potential or danger lies.

Sociality and Technology

To speak about "decisions" and to borrow this concept from social theory does not yet entail that there is any social intention behind their procedure. In the case of every micro-decision made on digital networks with the help of protocols, the power to make decisions has rather been taken out of the hands of human decision-makers and given to machines. The machines that carry out the decisions are of course produced and man- aged by people, who also determine and program their protocols and algorithms. Even the measures according to which decisions are made are necessarily established in protracted institutional negotiations. Yet, the great mass of micro-decisions can only be executed by computers, and it is this mass that underlies the technical definitions of the success of digital communication on computer-supported networks. They have become as effective as they are precisely because they circumvent the laborious human act of what could be called decision-making.

The act of deciding should not be confused with the process of choosing a possible answer by means of decision-making. It is dealt with by means of protocols and algorithms. In a technical and mathematical context, a de-cision (*Ent-Scheidung*) is also more than the execution of a predetermined protocol or programmed algorithm. Micro-decisions are in no way merely mechanical, determined, and therefore sub-complex processes. As interruptions, they are a fixed component of all communication on digital networks. Who can be connected with whom and who is disconnected from whom depend on these decisions. The precondition of every connection is its interruption.

Thus, instead of speaking about the technical determination of social processes or the precedence of social intentions before technical processes, the perspective followed here calls for a sort of procedural escalation, one that plays back and forth between automated execution and political interests, between the technical and the social. However important they might be to understanding digital cultures, descriptions of algorithms and protocols alone have not elucidated acts of decision-making so far. Such acts entail their own sort of politics and are not con-gruent with the commissions that establish protocols. A power analysis of present digital cultures should therefore operate in terms of technical infrastructures, their re-configurations of the social, and thus without drawing a line between human and technical actors.

At issue is thus not only how individuals are joined together by means of digital networks but also the capacity of these groups to act. Only by creating connections in networks and a type of connectivity based on material foundations is it possible for the sort of collectivity to develop that Eugene Thacker (2004) has referred to as an "aggregation of individuated units"—the kind that can organize itself for the sake of collective action. Connectivity is thus a precondition of collectivity, of intentional groups that are capable of action, but it does not inevitably result in collectivity. Thacker does not explicitly state the reverse side of his argument: The destruction of connectivity impairs collectivity. Who is connected with whom determines who can act in common. To determine the creation of disconnections or connections—to maintain or hinder them—is thus to exercise power, a sort of power that gains significance almost daily in light of the relations that are multiplied by digital media and the economic exploitation of these relations.

What so far might still sound schematic gains a degree of urgency if, as is the goal of this essay, one goes beyond examining the history of these networks in parallel with the history of political movements and their reconfigurations of the social (see, for instance, Baxmann et al. 2015). The challenges of pre-digital networks and their technologies also concerned the life-world (*Lebenswelt*), for they pertained to the manner in which people were connected with one another or disconnected from one another. Without question, the French Revolution can no less be separated from the printed pamphlet than the Arab Spring can be separated from Twitter and Facebook, albeit certainly not in a monocausal sense. Yet, while these familiar theses, in their grand claim to think about the intertwined nature of society and technology, oscillate between the poles of presumably neutral technology and outright techno-determinism, the focus of what follows will pertain to a different level, one that has been short-changed in recent theoretical discussions: My concern will be the places and times of micro-decisions about transmissions, the cultural techniques of synchronization that coordinate technical processes (see Kassung and Macho 2012), or, to be more specific, the infrastructures with which digital data packets are distributed on the Internet, connections and interruptions are produced, and networks are limited or broken down. From this history, it will become clear how much we know about the world and how much of what we are able to do is still being decided, prior to any content, at the level of technical media—but it should also become clear where their limits lie.

With its goal to examine the places and times of decision-making, this essay is meant for Internet activists and media historians, hackers and archaeologists, politicians and cultural theorists. Just as I intend to sketch the development of a political field, I also wish to illustrate that the history of a medium is always political and should not withdraw itself from the present that has emerged from it. That said, I nevertheless try to remain true to Georges Canguilhem's premise that epistemology always takes place among the rearguard (2006). We cannot confront the present because we are living in it. We may take action in it, appropriate it, and thus understand it. Yet, in doing so, we are not able to comprehend its epistemology, the orders of its knowledge. From a historical perspective, however, we can formulate a critique of the present without submitting ourselves unconditionally to the compulsion to be current that will make all of the circumstances of this book seem obsolete as soon as it is printed. According to Michel Foucault, a genealogy narrates the history of that which has come about and thus confronts what has become with its contingency: It is possible for everything to have been different, and it is possible that everything will be different (see Foucault 1997 and Saar 2008). To write a critique— even and particularly as regards the decisions that are being made about connections and disconnections—is therefore to create a space for that which is *not* inevitable and to invalidate what might seem to be a matter of course.

To speak about decisions also means to bear in mind that no decision is ineluctable and that every decision can be reached in a different manner—that it is possible to modify them for the better, but that they can also turn out for the worse. Yet even a bad decision is better than no decision, which leaves no room for improvement. To make decisions in advance or even to abolish the act of decision-making is, in every case, to reduce what is possible.

Control and Surveillance

Challenges to net neutrality and the revelation of seamless surveillance on the part of intelligence services, which are interconnected in ways that will be discussed below, have a technical, political, and epistemological dimension.[6] The objective of this chapter is to conceptualize these dimensions in an integrative manner. Actors as diverse as the EU Parliament, telecommunications providers, computer scientists, service providers, the FCC, Internet activists, hackers, and legal experts are negotiating the solution to a technical problem that has intervened with the Internet as an entity subject to politics—an entity,

6   Comments by media theorists about these debates have been rare, apart from those by Sebastian Gießmann, Dietmar Kammerer, Johannes Paßmann and Gregoire Chamayou (see Gießmann 2015, Kammerer 2015, Paßmann 2014, Chamayou 2015). This is surprising because, beyond the importance of these debates to daily politics, they are also of great theoretical interest; they refine central concepts such as surveillance, control, communication, or transmission and help to update them for the state of the twenty-first century. They illustrate where it is possible for historically-oriented media studies to intervene in current discussions and make its perspectives conducive to political critique.

therefore, that goes beyond distributing information but is also concerned with the order of distribution itself. To understand the collision of these aspects, it is necessary to examine the technical structure of the Internet, its transmission procedures, and the negotiation processes that have taken place in order to determine its architecture. Its origins will be discussed more extensively in the next chapter with reference to Paul Baran's model of a network. For this perspective, the calculation methods and algorithms used at the nodes and for the protocols are of little importance (they are also not commented upon in the historical texts consulted here). Of far greater significance are the network-architectonic questions concerning the layout of nodes, the distribution of data, and the production of connections. For it is only on this level that the tightly intertwined nature of technical solutions, political processes, and epistemological challenges will become clear.

End-to-End: The Architecture of Intermediacy

In simple terms, the various network architectures of the Internet are based on the fact that all transmitted data are graded into small, standardized packets, which each take various paths from node to node. At each node, the packets from various senders are processed according to the order of their arrival, and their further routes are determined in relation to the load of the network by means of the so-called header, which is analogous to a parcel label. No one has to plan or know which path a packet will take. Because traffic at the nodes is forwarded along without regard for its origin, the hardware being employed, and its content but rather exclusively according to the formalized manner provided by the protocol, users and service providers can thus be certain that data will arrive at their destination just as they have been sent. In principle, this process was conceived from the very beginning—that is, since the time of larger-scale capacities

per user before the development of the World Wide Web in
the 1990s—to be an open, equality-based, and fundamentally
non-discriminatory way of dealing with all packets. Even then,
however, this process was inscribed with the necessity of
organizing incoming packets at the nodes and of caring for the
management of their distribution.

What servers and routers are meant to accomplish at the nodes
was defined in 1973—nine years after Baran's publication and at
a time when providers were university-based computing centers
or research facilities—by the computer scientists Vinton Cerf and
Robert Kahn in their authoritative paper titled "A Protocol for
Packet Network Intercommunication" (Cerf and Kahn 1973). This
paper describes the still-valid rules for distribution known as the
Transmission Control Protocol (TCP), which puts data into the
form of a packet and supplies them with a readable header (see
Galloway 2004, 41 and, for a general introduction, Bunz 2009).
Developed at the same time, the *Internet Protocol* (IP) assigns
addresses to the packets, is responsible for routing the data
packets, and passes along incoming data from an application
to the network access of a given computer. Combined into TCP/
IP, the protocol ensures that, within a distributed network, all
or as many packets as possible will arrive at their destination.
It is essentially a so-called connectionless protocol, for it is
unnecessary to know whether a connection exists before a
transmission is sent. In connection-oriented processes, which
are used above all to manage telephone traffic, it is tested in
advance whether there is a direct connection to the transmission's destination. TCP serves to create this connection in the act
of transmission and during the transport itself, so that various
application protocols—such as the File Transfer Protocol (FTP),
the Simple Mail Transfer Protocol (SMTP), or the Hypertext

Transfer Protocol (HTTP)—are applicable across a network and multiple people can use the same line at once.[7]

According to the model presented by Cerf and Kahn, nodes operate as black boxes, simply and in an error-resistant manner, but they have no involvement with what passes through them on the basis of various types of hardware. In an influential article from 1984, the MIT computer scientists Jerome Saltzer, David Reed, and David Clark (everyone involved at this stage was male) referred to this structure as the "end-to-end principle." According to this principle, a network can "completely and correctly be implemented only with the knowledge and the help of the application standing at the end points of the communication system" (Saltzer et al. 1984, 287; see also Bendrath and Mueller 2010; Gillespie 2006). Conversely, this implies that only the programs at the terminals are responsible for processing and for maintaining the neutrality of the nodes, which alone possess the capacity for routing. In this sense, neutrality does not mean that no decisions are made but that they remain independent of the transmitted content and of the hardware being used on both sides.[8] Accordingly, as stated in 1984, the protocol does not determine the acts of decision-making but rather their set of rules.

The access allowed by the protocol is therefore restricted to the header and nothing can be implemented on the basis of the data in the body. In a Request for Comments (RFC) from 1996 (an RFC is an organizational, public document with which computer scientists coordinate and standardize the form of networks),

7   For the technical details of various protocol levels, see the helpful introduction by Jürgen Plate (2004).
8   Some providers, however, have done away with hardware neutrality by means of compulsory routers. For their own commercial interests, such providers allow particular models or functions, but only after a fee has been paid. In this regard it is also clear that the industry's openness to different types of hardware was driven by economic interests from the very beginning.

Brian Carpenter, a network engineer at CERN in Switzerland, described the end-to-end principle as an essential element of Internet architecture: "The network's job is to transmit datagrams as efficiently and flexibly as possible. Everything else should be done at the fringes" (1996). This principle, which was gradually refined, ensures that nodes can transport all packets independent of their assigned application, their content, the user in question, and the hardware being employed. What happens with the data in the packets is determined by the applications on the terminals. To summarize with three points, end-to-end allows for (1) flexibility with respect to technical solutions, because the nodes are not involved in computing processes; (2) the political freedom of content, because every participant can send anything; and finally (3) economic potential, because new services can develop without obstruction.

Because the intake and processing capacities of every node are technically limited, the threat exists, despite elaborate synchronization processes, that a transmission will be delayed or that packets will be lost when the network is overloaded. In accordance with the original protocol, packets are processed at the nodes as quickly as possible in the order of their arrival (this is known as the "best-effort principle"). When the number of arriving packets exceeds the availability of buffers or processing time, they will disappear or be discarded: "If all available buffers are used up, succeeding arrivals can be discarded since unacknowledged packets will be retransmitted" (Cerf and Kahn 1974, 645). This does not represent a problem because, within this model, the loss of packets is already taken into account: "No transmission can be 100 percent reliable" (ibid., 644). Since Baran's time, the redundancy of transmission has been the highest goal of every network model, and the idea was carried on by Cerf and Kahn: The network should remain operational not only if nodes are eliminated but also if individual packets are lost. Replacement deliveries are therefore requested automatically by the previous node if something is missing. The receiving node sends a confirmation for the packet to the previous node, and the digital copy on the output node is deleted. If no delivery confirmation is received, the packet is simply resent along a different route. However, in light of the vast amounts of data that have been increasing since the global spread of the Internet, noticeable delays can be experienced, even for the user at home, when the nodes are overloaded during periods of high traffic and requests are not even being sent.

Transmission Traffic Jams

The current debates predominantly revolve around how providers have been dealing with such traffic jams. Though the evocation of bottlenecks is part of a rhetoric of overload and most of the interested parties believe in it and benefit from it, the network rarely crashes. Apart from the possible overload and the background of regulation, the question of capacities of transmission leads to the center of technical challenges. Traffic jams stand in opposition to the potentially unlimited nature of digital data. In order to preserve the accustomed quality of transmissions, there are two options at our disposal. The first is expensive and comes with no guarantee of profit: to expand the infrastructures by further developing the network, which has been promoted in Germany by the Federal Ministry of Transport and Digital Infrastructure. The second option is to use the existing, suboptimal capacities in an optimized manner. Apparently it is more profitable to sell the present capacity at a higher price to those who are willing to pay for "fast lanes" and slow down the traffic for everyone else, something that Tim Berners-Lee, the developer of the World Wide Web, recently referred to as "bribery" (see Fung 2014). The goal of providers, as is clear to see in the case of Deutsche Telekom, is to make better use of the network by only slowly increasing its capacity, that is, to earn larger profits with merely marginal additional costs.

The problem that capacity traffic jams threaten the stable access
of all users on the network led the Chaos Computer Club (CCC)
to issue a moderate public statement: The prioritization of data
for the purpose of bandwidth management would be acceptable
"if this is made transparent to the customer, if it is stipulated in
the contract, and if in fact a capacity traffic jam exists, that is, if
the influence serves to allow all customers to have a fair portion
of the existing capacity" (2010). The CCC has drawn attention to
the fact that an insufficient infrastructural upgrade has led to
an increase of traffic jams and that sustainable action has to be
taken in response to this. Prioritization may be a poor solution,
but perhaps it might occasionally be necessary under transparent
conditions. Going beyond the position of the CCC, one could even
surmise that, in sufficiently complex data networks, it is in fact
the rule that capacity cannot keep up with use, and thus we have
a systemic problem on our hands.

Strictly speaking, the faltering network development at least in
Germany (faltering because there is a lack of incentive) has on
its own ensured a sort of sustainable net neutrality because
neutrality is not a problem if there is sufficient capacity. Its
endorsement implies an endorsement for the improvement
of infrastructures, which poses its own set of questions and
problems: Who will finance them and to whom will they belong?
What power will materialize in them and on what legal basis can
they be democratically appropriated? For, as has been known
since the nineteenth century, the development of large infrastructural networks requires an uncanny accumulation of capital.
Networks of power, which the historian of technology Thomas
P. Hughes described in his monumental work on the rise of the
large American electricity companies, are too tightly entangled
with the rise of capitalism (1993). It is hardly novel to remark
that the development of infrastructures invites conflict. In the
case of network development alone, which is unquestionably
momentous and inevitable, it seems unlikely that this solution

will solve the many challenges that go beyond the mere management of bandwidth.

It has become increasingly difficult, moreover, to interpret the interests of the individual actors involved. Neutrality, as has already become clear, lies in the hands of the providers, whereas lawmakers around the world have been asked to create legal frameworks (see Marsden 2010). However, in light of the NSA scandal and the evident cooperation of many providers with intelligence services, this division of labor has become somewhat diffuse. Providers make their own rules and states such as China or the United States, colluding with the providers, monitor large swaths of traffic in a way that can hardly be called neutral. This is all the more reason to try to understand what is at stake with net neutrality.

The concept of net neutrality was coined by Tim Wu in a series of legal and political debates.[9] Together with the constitutional lawyer Lawrence Lessig, Wu was intensively engaged with the political issues and the technical challenges of net neutrality in order to shift the discussion away from judicial matters toward questions of civil rights (Wu 2003; see also van Schewick 2010). According to Wu's definition, net neutrality guarantees that, within a network, all types of information are transmitted equally and the widest variety of applications can be supported, which would enable democratic participation in the social processes that are based on it. For Wu, net neutrality is therefore embedded in the structure of the Internet, in which images, texts, and sounds are processed independently: "The principle suggests that information networks are often more valuable when they are less specialized, when they are a platform for multiple use" (2015).

9   Before becoming a professor at Columbia Law School, Wu was employed by a company devoted to deep packet inspection (2009). In 2014, he was a candidate in the Democratic primary for lieutenant governor in the state of New York.

The debates taking place in North America are frequently concerned with economic issues. Net neutrality is promoted in the name of not hindering the Internet's potential for innovation (read: profit) by eliminating online advertising.[10] The fear is that large providers could exploit their position as gatekeepers in order to impede or block competition, a fear that was recently substantiated by the much-discussed case of T-Mobile blocking Skype from its mobile network.[11] Competition is especially fierce in the sector of mobile Internet devices because wireless data transmission, on account of the radio spectrum, has physically limited capacities that cannot be expanded. For this reason, the providers of such services have long been selective about what type of traffic is given preferential treatment on mobile networks. For example, the use of fee-based streaming services such as Spotify is frequently not counted as part of a customer's data plan. Terms of use can thus cut access to the Internet. There have likewise been attempts to involve the main commercial contributors to so much traffic—most notably Google, YouTube, and Netflix—in paying for the costs of the infrastructures that they benefit from but neglect to finance. Providers plan on charging for giving advertisers access to customers. What remains to be decided in all of this is the nature of the relationship between the owners of the infrastructure and those who use it—the user, on the one hand, and the provider on the other.[12]

10   For an overview of the economic and legal issues, see Krämer et al. (2013) and Martini (2011). It is noteworthy that these texts neglect to discuss the controversial surveillance that has taken place by means of deep packet inspection.

11   The transmission of voices, which I will return to below, is especially susceptible to fluctuations in transmission quality because it tolerates neither delays in the transmission ("latency") nor irregular sequences of arriving data packets ("jitters"). The inconsistency of Skype conversations demonstrates this quite clearly. More than that of other types of content, the transmission of voices and video relies on a rigid sort of time management to guarantee the impression of being present.

12   On the legal and political dimensions of these developments, see the interim report by the project group devoted to net neutrality as part of the German

In this regard, Lessig has stressed the economic and cultural benefits of open networks extensively (see Lessig 2004; Mueller 2004). As far as he is concerned, it is precisely by being neutral that the Internet can generate new markets that are meant to be accessible to everyone in a free society. In his opinion, it is only in exceptional cases, such as Internet television or Voice over IP services (VoIP) for the police or military, that it is sensible for providers to abolish neutrality. This is because such services can only maintain their standards with stable connections and would thus be at a disadvantage in comparison with other types. In other words, some sort of special status should be accorded to infrastructure that is critical. That said, a general limitation on traffic would contradict Metcalfe's Law, according to which the value of a network is proportional to the number of possible connections between its users, whereby the costs of the network remain proportional merely to its number of users.[13] If hierarchies come to prevail between a network's nodes, the value of this network will decrease.

As Wu's and Lessig's interventions have repeatedly pointed out, the question of whether data packets should be treated unequally on the Internet is a matter that, beyond economic issues, concerns the democratic conception of the Internet, which in turn is based on the end-to-end principle. Proponents of net neutrality frequently draw conclusions about the freedom of expression and economic prosperity on the basis of the technical conditions of the Internet itself. In Lessig's words, "This imposed neutrality about how the wires would be used left the field open for others to use the wires in ways no one ever expected. The

government's investigative committee on the Internet and digital society (*Enquete-Kommission Internet und digitale Gesellschaft*; Deutscher Bundestag 2012). Employing the methodology of Science and Technology Studies, Sebastian Gießmann (2015) has investigated the various forms of collaboration that, within the framework of this committee, brought about the demand for net neutrality and infrastructural-political standards.

13   This law, which was suggested in the late 1980s by Robert Metcalfe, was first properly formulated in 1993 by George Gilder (2000).

internet was one such way" (2004, 149). The absence of an over-
arching authority for making decisions and the detachment of
protocols from institutional authority in general can be understood as an opportunity for democratic organization and for
carrying out Article 19 of the UN's Universal Declaration of Human
Rights. The latter not only calls for the freedom of expression; it
also endorses the right "to seek, receive and impart information
and ideas through any media and regardless of frontiers" (United
Nations 1948).

The debates of recent years have been ignited by the fact that
the infrastructures necessary for the Internet have come to form
the foundation of a new type of public sphere. As such, their
social value is greater than the business interests of the private
companies that own them. It is rather difficult to reconcile their
pursuit of profit with the maintenance of these structures, which
are so vital to modern society. As the media theorist Johannes
Paßmann has shown, such an understanding of net neutrality is
the continuation of the dream, which is enormously important
to the constitution of the Internet, of establishing a democratic
medium, something similar to what was expressed in John Perry
Barlow's emailed Internet manifesto from 1996. At that time, the
Internet promised to be an open and democratic social order
that, like today, had to be protected from the potential influences
of private business. According to Paßmann (2014), today's
recourse to these positions implicitly maintains that something
like neutral use could even exist and that a neutral market situation could even be conceivable, which, in light of the dominant
position of the large companies, is hardly the case. Put simply, we
are now facing a conflict over the distribution of resources, and
this conflict will determine who can be connected with whom and
who will know anything about it.

The proclaimed fear that all data packets will no longer be
sent without discrimination by all providers consists primarily,
according to the activists at Netzpolitik.org or La Quadrature du
Net, in the fact that private companies will decide what will be

transmitted and what will not. It is around this question of sovereignty that Halpin's idea of an "immaterial civil war" revolves. The reverse side of prioritization is discrimination. This is so because, first, less bandwidth will be available to non-prioritized users and, second, because the possibility of various sorts of surveillance, control, and obstruction will thus appear on the horizon. According to activists, the long-term consequence of abolishing net neutrality would be to forfeit the democratic function of the Internet, which they claim to be a fundamental component of the open society of the twenty-first century and, as is especially argued in North America, a precondition for the innovative potential of new services and thus of the economic dimension of networking.[14] From this perspective, net neutrality serves the common good.

The counterargument from industry is that, in light of the increasing amount of data traffic, it is only by controlling and regulating transmissions that a satisfactory user experience on the Internet will even be possible. In an internal memo from 2010 entitled *What Does Net Neutrality Really Mean?*, Deutsche Telekom mentions "innovative network management" and "different classes of quality," the goal of which is to enhance the "quality of services" and to promote "an efficient use of network resources." In metaphorical terms, the congestion of the data highway should be countered by a traffic control system that not only makes use of signs to ensure the flow of traffic but also inspects the occupants of the cars in order to see who has to reach his or her destination more quickly—ambulances and vehicles carrying hazardous materials will be given priority by the authorities, while paying customers will be given priority over those unwilling to pay.[15] Out of the need, brought about by increasing volume,

---

14   My attention here is restricted to the debates that have been taking place in Western Europe and North America. For a more broadly international comparison, see Bertscheck et al. (2013).

15   Of course, this metaphor is anything but innocent, but it already presents a solution in the form of toll roads.

not only to control but also regulate data traffic, providers
are abandoning the practice of treating everything equally
and instead giving preference to those who are willing to pay
more. For everyone involved, however, the price (or the profit)
is that the content of every car and every data packet will have
to be inspected in order for this act of selection to take place.
Prioritization—and this point is central—entails that the decisions
made at nodes will be based on the providers' knowledge about
what is being transmitted.

Deep Packet Inspection

There are a number of reasons why these debates have res-
onated so strongly and why they have been carried out so
vehemently not only among lawyers and economists but also,
for some years, online. First, and as shown above, their historical
location lies in the large-scale spread of volume-independent
tariffs and flat fees, which, in a mixed calculation, offsets the
intensive use of certain users against the more minimal use
of others. The primary causes of this explosion of traffic have
been peer-to-peer applications such as Bittorrent or eMule,
the steadily increasing amounts of data required by cloud-
based services and online gaming, the increase of spam, and
the growing popularity of fluctuation-sensitive services such as
video telephony, streaming, or the convergence of television and
the Internet.[16] This, in turn, is likewise dependent on a technical
necessity: The transmission of an email is less time-critical than
that of a video call. The latter has to arrive on time at its destination in order to minimize interruption. Among other interested parties, medical services and law enforcement agencies
have thus repeatedly demanded that quality assurances be

16   See Blumenthal and Clark (2001). It has been suggested, moreover, that
     streaming services should abandon packet switching and return to using
     line-based transmission, which does not rely on individual packets running
     through various nodes but rather on a single connection that would save
     energy and processing time (see Sietmann 2011).

established by giving priority to such services. To the extent that these services are subject to commercial interests and their providers stand to earn profits from them, however, the latter are confronted with a homemade problem. It has become more and more evident that the architecture of the Internet is not suitable for video services, which are based on the principle of broadcasting, that is, on distributing the same content to multiple users. Because of insufficient investments in development, too, it is inevitable that the infrastructure will be overloaded for a long time to come.

The conflict, however, has not yet reached the point where it is simply a matter of private providers clashing with public interests. This is because, second, processes of deep packet inspection have been perfected in recent years that, in addition to the big-data analysis of metadata, allow for a more effective means of regulating traffic than is possible by treating all packets equally.[17] Referred to as the "body scanner for the Internet" by the computer scientist Rüdiger Weis (2012), deep packet inspection, which is a collective term for a variety of technologies, goes far beyond solving the congestion problems of the network. At the nodes, that is, where transmissions are interrupted, it allows the content of data packets to be inspected at a bit-level of accuracy. Instead of relying on headers to identify data packets, it enables bit packets to be opened and their so-called "payload" to be read and analyzed individually or statistically. The political and Internet activist Markus Beckedahl has thus declared deep packet inspection to be a "risky technology" that entails, even if sensible quality assurances are instituted, the possibility of seamless surveillance (see Siering 2011).

In the case of stateful packet inspection, which remains common, every data packet is identified and allocated according to its

---

17 On the differences between these various processes and on their legal foundations, see Bedner (2009). On the advantages and disadvantages of using deep packet inspection to manage networks, see Bärwolff (2009).

header. In the presently used transmission protocol IPv4, the header can admittedly be marked with information about the importance of a packet, but there are no standards or obligations for providers to prioritize these packets (see Beckedahl 2009). With the gradual introduction of IPv6, which has been going on for a few years (IPv5 was leapfrogged), the classification of transport types (but also the encryption of content) that was not implemented with IPv4 has become possible. This has facilitated the prioritization of individual packets without the use of deep packet inspection (see Deutscher Bundestag 2012). However, because all of the large providers have meanwhile acquired the hardware necessary for deep packet inspection—on account of legal provisions to be explained later, providers in the United States have even been required to acquire this hardware—and because there has been enough incentive to regulate traffic even beyond the issue of pure bandwidth management, it would be premature to place too much faith in this simple solution.

Every data packet consists of multiple sequential but independent logistical layers, the purpose of which is to enable communication between different networks. A data packet has several casings, so to speak, each of which bears a different sort of information (Figure 1). At a given node, the upper layers have to be exposed in order for a packet to be distributed further, because these layers contain transportation-oriented data. They provide information about the hardware and the header to be used for making the connection and transmission, information that is required for TCP/IP to operate. Transmissions made by means of these protocols have access only to these upper layers. The data kept in the lower layers are admittedly present but, even without encryption, they cannot readily be accessed during the application of the protocol. Depending on the hardware and provider being used, however, deep packet inspection also allows for the application-oriented layers to be read—from the layer containing transmitted information for a given browser application, to the layer dealing with the peer-to-peer client, all the way to that concerned with Skype. To this end, devices are equipped with data signatures with which traffic is scanned, classified, and further processed. Because deep packet inspection analyzes all aspects of traffic, the latest hardware must therefore be able to perform at a far higher level than conventional network technology, which only processes headers. This occurs during the brief interruptions when decisions are made about the subsequent routes to be taken. With the knowledge gained by means of deep packet inspection, it is now possible, within the same window of time, to open other layers and to modify these decisions accordingly (see Królikowski 2014; Bar-Yanai et al. 2010). The conditions have changed to the extent that the new technology has infiltrated the time and place of decision-making.

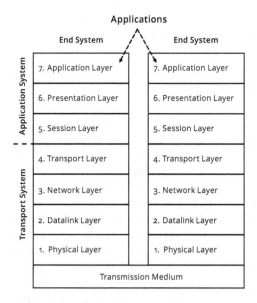

[Figure 1] OSI-Model (Source: Wikimedia)

A variety of parties happen to be interested in such processes: Internet providers use this technology for bandwidth management or for filtering out email spam, fee-based service providers use it to measure sales volume, the police use it to fight crime, lawyers working for the entertainment industry use it to prosecute illegal downloads, and it is valuable to online commerce as a means to create personalized advertising. It is employed in corporate networks to secure outgoing data and is used in a simplified form in firewalls and spam filters, which can function without blocking IP or DNS-addresses (see Ingham and Forrest 2002). Deep packet inspection has also become a common tool employed by intelligence services and can serve as a weapon in cyber warfare. In China, Iran, and Turkey, for instance, deep packet inspection is applied to analyze online search queries with certain keywords as well as to prevent access, at the nodes, to websites such as YouTube or Twitter (see Human Rights Watch 2014). As a branch of the Pentagon, the NSA also makes use of it (among other processes) to preselect, at the providers' nodes, that which the agency wishes to save and evaluate in the interest of national security (see Bamford 2012).

One could go so far as to claim that the practices of the NSA and other intelligence services would not be possible without these technologies, which thus turn out to be rather Janus-faced: That which is meant to facilitate the fair distribution of network capacity can be used for the sake of surveillance and oppression. As a stage of escalation, the processes of deep packet inspection can consequently be cited to demonstrate how the debates about net neutrality and NSA surveillance, despite all their differences, converge at a technical level: The objectives of both sides are achieved during the interruptions of transmissions and thus depend on the micro-temporality of decisions.

While deep packet inspection, which is technically sophisticated and requires large amounts of computing, enables the contents of data packets to be read, statistical or stochastic packet inspection enables their patters to be analyzed statistically and thus selected and, if appropriate, further processed. Because there are methods of encryption to prevent the inspection of packets (that is, to prevent their contents from being read), processes have been developed to block individual ports or to identify, by analyzing the patterns of transmitted packets and their so-called metadata, various applications in order to pinpoint or even block certain peer-to-peer applications that are bandwidth-intensive and frequently used for illegal downloads. If numerous small packets are being sent at regular intervals, this implies the use of VoIP or the continuous use of full peer-to-peer bandwidth, whereas emails course through the line at an irregular rate (see McKelvey 2010; Sietmann 2011; Sandvig 2007). Such patterns can accordingly be recognized by big-data analysis, which extracts and algorithmically evaluates information directly from collected data, and their volumes can be technically limited or their causes can be detected. The popularity of these systems is also suggested by the fact that, since 2014, standards for exchanging data between different types of hardware have been established (see International Telecommunication Union 2012).

For several years, the processes of deep packet inspection have been implemented on a hardware-basis by a variety of producers. Because of the legal gray area surrounding their use, however, it is not easy to obtain more precise information about their basic principles. In comparison with the long-available systems for monitoring the nodes of telephone networks, the essential difference lies in the sheer capacity of data that can be processed and in the possibility of processing such data with graph-based analytic methods. For example, once it is integrated into a network node, the flagship model of Cisco's Service Control Engines, the SCE 10000, is able to monitor, track, and manage twenty million simultaneous sessions of up to two million concurrent subscribers with a maximum throughput of sixty gigabits per second.[18] Users do not even notice that this is taking place:

18   In Russia, where such devices are not commercially available, they can be purchased on the black market for approximately $150,000 (see Used Cisco Info 2015).

With this platform, providers can identify content trans-
ported over any protocol, provide detailed analysis and
control of complex content-based applications, and prioritize
sessions in real time. . . . With this exclusive, high-perform-
ance, stateful architecture, operators have better capabilities
for profitably delivering an array of services customized to
individual subscriber needs. (Cisco Systems 2015)

Although this advertisement on Cisco's homepage foregrounds
the needs of the users whose traffic is to be monitored and
controlled, the situation came to a head at the legal level: The
rejected Stop Online Piracy Act (SOPA), a bill introduced in the
US House of Representatives in 2011, and the failed international
Anti-Counterfeiting Trade Agreement (ACTA), both of which
succumbed to considerable public pressure, would have forced
providers to use such hardware to filter search queries for the
transmission of copyright-protected contents and to collect
the corresponding IP addresses (see Halpin 2013, 10). Access to
allegedly illegal websites would thus have been blocked, net neutrality would have been broken, and all of this would have been
legally mandated at the international level.

As Constanze Kurz of the Chaos Computer Club has pointed
out, it can be presumed that the hardware being used in coun-
tries such as Turkey, China, Syria, or Iran is considerably more
powerful (see Kurz 2011). Several hundred documents leaked by
WikiLeaks under the name "Spyfiles," which consist largely of
product presentations and operating instructions by Western
security firms, demonstrate the potential applications that such
technologies have for governments. In addition to employing
deep and statistical packet inspection, the possibility of creating
graphs between generated profiles, which is frequently being
integrated into devices, allows these technologies to identify
people and their networks (see Lemke 2008). As one of many
examples, the system known as Eagle Glint, which is produced
by the French company Amesys, can monitor approximately four
terabytes of data and calculate profiles out of this information

(see Sonne and Gauthier-Villars 2012; WikiLeaks 2011). In 2013, five Libyan dissidents filed a complaint against the company because its technology was used to identify them by Gaddafi's regime, which arrested and tortured them (see Worldwide Human Rights Movement 2013). As Dietmar Kammerer has shown, however, a legally-binding international ban on exporting surveillance and espionage hardware does not exist—not least because Western intelligence services have come to rely on these technologies as well (2015).

With such hardware, with deep packet inspection, and with the mathematical methods of graph theory, it has become quite easy to monitor the unencrypted traffic of individual users in a selective manner, to identify their friends and connections, and even at times to manipulate their access to data. In this regard it is not only interesting what someone is communicating but also to whom it is being communicated, how long the communication lasts, from where it is being sent, and how frequently it occurs. Metadata can potentially contain information that is in fact more important than the contents of the message—but above all they can be analyzed automatically in large quantities, which is not the case with contents. They cannot be encrypted but rather, at best, they can be concealed by means of something like a Tor network, which makes connection data anonymous.[19] Even encrypted packets, in which the lower layers of the payload are inaccessible, can be analyzed by means of statistical or stochastic packet inspection. The technologies used for such inspection are initiated where connections are produced between people—be it by them staying at places that can be localized (by means of transmission towers) or by the contacts that they have cultivated

---

19   Tor is an acronym for "The Onion Router." In a network of this sort, which was developed by the US Navy, traffic is directed through diverse and inter-nationally dispersed intermediary stations and is thus difficult to identify. The process, however, slows the traffic down, which in turn renders time-critical services dysfunctional.

online.[20] Surveillance is initiated where these connections are
produced by means of the interruptions that are needed for
decisions to be made, namely at the nodes of the network. It
takes place during the time that these interruptions last.

However, it is not only the terror of such regimes but also the
efforts of providers to transmit various sorts of traffic at various
speeds that depend on the big-data analysis of metadata and
on the possibilities afforded by deep packet inspection: When
the point has been reached where providers are capable of dis-
tinguishing between data packets with text or video data, it will
then be sensible to treat the latter with priority. Even if providers
and intelligence services have different definitions of what "contents" are, they have taken identical paths on the way to reaching
their respective definitions. As Lawrence Lessig has pointed out
(2004, 174), it is not yet the case that the need to control data
transmissions will necessarily result in the establishment of
secretive or high-profit monopolies over the transmission of data.
And yet whenever control is necessary, surveillance is possible.

"Collecting It All"

In terms of network management, control is necessary
for maintaining traffic, but it also entails the possibility of
surveillance. Technically speaking, surveillance in digital networks
is often just a parasite living off of the necessary controls; it is
something that is freeloading off of neutrality.

The revelations leaked by the whistleblower Edward Snowden,
who was twenty-nine years old at the time, made it irrefutably
known to the global public that intelligence services around the
world are attempting to tap into *all* data packets, that they are

20   In 2010, the computer scientist Jens-Martin Loebel began an experimental
      diary in which he recorded all of his GPS data. Even from the data collected
      over the course of a few weeks, Loebel was able to make exact predictions
      about his behavior, that is, about his presence at particular places at
      particular times (2011).

doing so with the means described above (among others), and that they are doing so with or without any justifiable suspicions about terrorist or criminal activity. With evidence from top-secret documents it became obvious that big data are now married to a misguided security policy to form a dream couple in our society of control.[21] It is no surprise, then, that one of the slogans used by Keith Alexander, a former director of the NSA, was "collecting it all" (cited by Greenwald [2014, 79] from an internal NSA memorandum). Consequently, the entire population of the world is being held under general suspicion. The technical condition behind the NSA's role is that decisions have to be made about every data packet and that, to this end, every one of them has to be buffered for a brief moment. The extent of the subsequent automated surveillance is an effect of the architecture of digital networks. The place of decision-making during the time of interruption is the main gateways at which the necessary act of control is placed side-by-side with the act of surveillance. They dwarf any of the manual efforts made by the Stasi or other historical secret services. To summarize in polemic terms: All conspiracy theories are true.

Even if much of what the leaked documents have made public has long been known and even if Snowden has sacrificed his life, as the IT security expert Sandro Gaycken has remarked, simply to reveal the long-presumed evidence of an "open secret" (2013), the importance of the findings cannot be stressed enough. Across national borders and continents, the documents call into question the legitimacy of the institutions involved. While it might have been known that the NSA aims to achieve the most efficient means of surveillance, the conspicuous presence of the logos of companies such as Facebook, Google, or Apple in internal documents underscores this knowledge. The risk is that the uncovered quantity of surveillance will overshadow its political

21 On Snowden, see Lyon (2014) and the collection of newspaper articles and blog entries in Beckedahl and Meister (2014), which explore the social and political side of the affair but largely ignore its technological aspects.

significance, while little will be learned about the technologies that have been used. The political dimension of the affair goes beyond the unquestionably important debates about privacy and beyond reviving the discussion of WikiLeaks as a safe haven for whistleblowers (Steinmetz 2012). Of greater concern are the disconnections and connections of communication and the constitution of the social, which, under the aegis of seamless surveillance, has been placed on a new foundation.

As early as 1982, James Bamford provided extensive descriptions of the NSA's practices in his book *The Puzzle Practice*, and he updated his oberservations in the more recent *The Shadow Factory* (2008). Such practices have similarly been denounced, but not irrefutably substantiated, by the whistleblowers Thomas Drake and William Binney. Even Friedrich Kittler, following Bamford's lead in the 1980s, made reference to the NSA's clandestine technology (Kittler 1986/2014). Despite the ambivalent reactions to the leaks—some concocted grand conspiracy theories, others saw them as a threat to public life[22]—it was Snowden's documents that permanently altered the tableau of activity and our trust in the position of everyone involved. Not least, the documents also clearly exposed the relevance of micro-decisions. Boundless surveillance and total transparency, which were actively pursued and which for a long time were opposed only by practical limitations, have considerably increased the potency of decision-making because they perpetuate an imbalance of power relations: Whoever invisibly controls things behind the scenes also has control over who knows or does not know anything about surveillance. And whoever is ignorant of the fact that he or she is under suspicion is consequently unable to protest.

Behind the debates spurred by Snowden lies the convergence, legally promoted in the United States since the 1970s, of security

22 Nigel Inkster, the former director of the British Secret Intelligence Service, attempted to relativize Snowden's leaks from the perspective of intelligence agencies (2014).

and information technologies, which has only escalated since the introduction of the Internet. In a speech delivered to the Brookings Institution—"Going Dark: Are Technology, Piracy, and Public Safety on a Collision Course?"—the Federal Bureau of Investigation's (FBI's) director James Comey, reacting to Snowden's leaks, openly discussed the difficulties that his colleagues have faced in their efforts to keep up with technological developments: "We have the legal authority to intercept and access communications and information pursuant to court order, but we often lack the technical ability to do so" (2014). The challenge in fighting crime, he noted, is that of keeping pace with the ever-changing pathways of communication, given that a suspect might have parallel access to a land-line telephone, a mobile phone, instant messaging, and Voice over IP. Comey therefore suggested that a public discussion should take place regarding the uses and drawbacks of digital encryption. Tellingly, he gave his speech shortly after Apple's announcement that its new iPhone models would be equipped with a type of encryption that Apple itself, according to the company's own claims, is unable to decode (Apple 2015). No less significant is the fact that both Comey and Apple exempt cloud services from the security afforded by encryption; state institutions will still have access to them for the purpose of preventing crime. It must therefore be asked, as Comey stated, whether it would truly be desirable to encrypt the vast majority of transmitted communication, given that this would immensely impede law enforcement and create large costs. Public interest is thus being played off against the right to privacy: "Justice may be denied, because of a locked phone or an encrypted hard drive" (2014).

The background of the debate initiated by Comey is occupied largely by the Communication Assistance for Law Enforcement Act (CALEA), which was passed in 1994 during Bill Clinton's presidency. According to this law, all providers of communication services in the United States—companies with the "capability for generating, acquiring, storing, transforming, processing, retrieving, utilizing or making available information via telecommunications" (US Congress 1996)—must embed in their products the possibility of monitoring communication for purposes of assisting legally sanctioned police investigations. Analogously, according to Statute 110 of the German Telecommunications Law (*Telekommunikationsgesetz*), providers are likewise obligated to cooperate with law enforcement during criminal prosecutions. The objective of the American law is "to make clear a telecommunications carrier's duty to cooperate in the interception of communications for law enforcement purposes, and for other purposes" (US Congress 1996). That final clause leaves plenty of room for interpretation. By means of a few amendments, the law covers, in addition to traditional telephone and Internet providers, Voice-over-IP providers as well. Even at the level of hardware, they have to modify their services in such a surveillance-friendly manner that it is possible for institutions to use them for the continuous surveillance of potential criminals, provided that a court order has been issued to do so. American providers are therefore only permitted to use routers and servers that are technically suitable for surveillance. This does not necessarily mean that they are equipped for deep packet inspection but that they must include traditional methods for eavesdropping (compared to which, however, deep packet inspection represents a massive technical simplification).

It became known as early as 2007 that the FBI, using a system called the Digital Collection System Network (DCSNet) and with full support of the law, has been able to monitor, comprehensively, the telephonic communication of potential criminals at the nodes of telecommunications providers. In doing so, however, the Bureau is only able to register connections and metadata; it cannot inspect the contents of communication (see Singel 2007). In 2010, a proposed amendment to the law was overturned that would have forced Internet companies such as Facebook or Google to integrate the possibility of institutional surveillance into their instant-messaging services—even if it was

58   later exposed that these companies, too, share their data with the NSA (see Savage 2013).

In sum, this means that both hardware and software have to be equipped to enable surveillance. Yet, as Comey stressed, the FBI can hardly keep up with the speed of technological innovation. On account of encryption, the agency is finding itself in an increasingly awkward situation, and this is also the case because providers are not always willing to cooperate in a satisfactory manner: "I want people to understand that law enforcement needs to be able to access communications and information to bring people to justice" (2014). In Comey's estimation, security and privacy, which some providers would like to guarantee for their customers, are a hindrance to law enforcement, and encryption can only be justified if there also happens to be a back door for "lawful interceptions" by the FBI. It is never mentioned that this back door might also be of service to certain interested parties that are somewhat less virtuous. A few days after Comey's speech, the Electronic Frontier Foundation (EFF), which fights to protect civil liberties in the digital age and is also an active participant in the debates about net neutrality, issued a response in which it claimed that the FBI should be trying to safeguard the security of everyone instead of encouraging providers to offer less security to their customers (C. Cohn 2014).

With the goal of securely verifying online transactions, the US government attempted as early as 1993 to introduce a hardware-based standard encryption for all networked devices. This encryption also would have allowed those involved in a given transaction to be identified unambivalently.[23] Encryption notwithstanding, the algorithm known as Skipjack, which was to be used by the Clapston and Clipper chips installed in all

23   On the debates over encryption and decryption in the United States during the mid-1990s (the so-called Crypto Wars), see Engemann (2015). Regarding the history of encryption and its conflict with the state, see Diffie and Landau (2010).

network-compatible devices, would have nevertheless provided the government with a steady opportunity to monitor the exchange of data. The promise was more or less this: We will provide you with security if you provide us, and only us, with access to your privacy. It was intended for the key to all encrypted devices to be kept not only by the user but also in a government database, where retrieval was only possible by court order. These efforts ultimately failed on account of public pressure and protests from companies worrying about foreign markets. It was methods such as these, however, that the NSA revived without any legal basis but simply as a component of the War on Terror. Comey has reheated this debate from the 1980s and has made it clear just how little the government's skeptical position on encryption has changed. He has also revealed, however, the immense measures that the FBI alone has since taken to enable decryption and surveillance.

There is more to this discussion than the mere desire to create better working conditions for investigators. The CALEA law also implies that a provider is not responsible for decoding an encryption applied by a user. This task is reserved for the law enforcement authorities. In fact, Comey's argumentation suggests that in the future providers should be forced, with the help of deep packet inspection, to avoid processing encrypted traffic at all. Encryption, according to this argument, should simply be prohibited outright in order to inhibit those who have something to hide.

Even beyond the economic disadvantages that American providers have already faced upon the introduction of the law, the weak points of Comey's argumentation are obvious: He is silent, for instance, about how the FBI should go about protecting its own data exchanges. To demand that a technical threshold be put in place that fundamentally prohibits encryption seems both naïve and dangerous for all who, with good reason, want to protect their online traffic—from bankers to human rights activists to police officers themselves. Instead, Comey's suggestion insinuates that anyone who uses encryption to safeguard his or her privacy from the NSA and data-hungry companies—and not simply to conceal crimes—is implicitly in favor of obstructing justice. It does not seem unrealistic to suppose that the next step would be to make any opposition to the NSA or the FBI illegal—and to make it illegal, too, to discuss their activities in public.

Even though the FBI and the NSA cannot be treated as a single entity, Comey's argumentation has made it clear how extensively the issue of net neutrality has been scrutinized by government agencies. His remarks perfectly complement the practices of the NSA, which for many years did not feel subjected to the limitations imposed on the FBI. Unlike that of the FBI, however, the NSA's goal is simply to collect, independent of any legal authority, all available data in order to fight global terrorism. There have been indications, however, that it is also engaged in industrial espionage and politically motivated acts of eavesdropping. In contrast to the FBI, the intelligence services determine on their own who is or who is not an enemy of the state. The main problem faced by the NSA, however, is not encryption but rather the difficulty of storing vast amounts of information in light of the so-called three Vs of big data— "volume, velocity, and variety" (Bamford 2008, 331). In his first interview with the journalists Laura Poitras, Glenn Greenwald, and Ewen MacAskill, which took place in June of 2013, Edward Snowden made the following remarks: "It ingests them by default. It collects them in its system and it filters them and it analyzes them and it measures them and it stores them for periods of time simply because that is the easiest, most efficient, and most valuable way to achieve these ends" (Greenwald et al. 2013).

A few days before this interview, in which Snowden, who before going into hiding had been an infrastructure analyst for the defense contractor Booz Allen Hamilton, identified himself as a whistleblower, the British newspaper *The Guardian* published the first document from a batch of more than two hundred thousand:

a secret order from the Foreign Intelligence Surveillance Court. **61**
The latter was established in the 1970s in response to the illegal
monitoring of human rights activists and pacifists; its task is to
review requests for surveillance warrants, and it later became an
extension of the NSA.[24] As of 2012, the court had received more
than twenty thousand requests for such warrants, of which it
rejected only eleven (Greenwald 2014, 95). In the first leaked document, the provider Verizon is issued the following order, which
appears somewhat ironically under the header "TOP SECRET//SI//
NOFORN" (for Special Intelligence, No Foreign Nationals):

> It is hereby ordered that, the Custodian of Records shall
> produce to the National Security Agency (NSA) upon service
> of this Order, and continue production on an ongoing
> daily basis thereafter for the duration of this Order, unless
> otherwise ordered by the Court, an electronic copy of the
> following tangible things: all call detail records or 'telephony
> metadata' created by Verizon for communications (i)
> between the United States and abroad; or (ii) wholly within
> the United States, including local telephone calls. . . . It is
> further ordered that no person shall disclose to any other
> person that the FBI or NSA has sought or obtained tangible
> things under this Order . . . (quoted from *Guardian* 2013)

The bottom line of the document states the date of declas-
sification: April 12, 2038. The only way to protest against a secret
order such as this is to do so before a secret court.[25] There is, in
other words, no way to protest at all.

The way that the revelations unfolded was staged according to a
tightly orchestrated strategy: One day after this document had
informed the global public that the largest Internet provider in

---

24 The aftermath of the Snowden revelations will only be given marginal
    attention here. For a comprehensive treatment of the affair, see Landau
    (2013; 2014). On Snowden's role as a whistleblower, see Scheuerman (2014).

25 The new role of secrecy in digital cultures has been described by Timon
    Beyes and Claus Pias (2014).

the United States has to pass along *all* of its communication data to the NSA, what followed was the release of a strikingly low-quality internal PowerPoint presentation meant to train people on how to use the espionage program Planning Tool for Resource Integration, Synchronization, and Management (PRISM). Within this presentation, Microsoft, Yahoo, Google, Facebook, PalTalk, YouTube, Skype, AOL, and Apple are mentioned as providers whose server data are routinely collected. As the slides indicate, the NSA has access to all the processes conducted on these platforms, to all the content saved there, and to Voice-over-IP conversations (see Electronic Frontier Foundation 2013). The leaks released shortly thereafter concerned the software XKeys-core, which allows the Internet traffic of a targeted person to be monitored live. Going beyond the scope of CALEA, it forces providers to share with the NSA the data that they have collected about all of their users, not simply their data about suspected criminals. In an interview on German television, Snowden described the capabilities of the program as follows:

> You could read anyone's email in the world, anybody you've got an email address for. Any website: You can watch traffic to and from it. Any computer that an individual sits at: You can watch it. Any laptop that you're tracking: you can follow it as it moves from place to place throughout the world. It's a one-stop-shop for access to the NSA's information. (Mestmacher-Steiner 2014)

More and more new documents were brought to light in the subsequent weeks, and they evidenced the extent to which surveillance and espionage are being conducted not only by the NSA but also by the British intelligence agency GCHQ (especially by means of its Tempora computer program) and by the intelligence services of nearly every Western industrialized nation. They demonstrated, in other words, the dissolution of privacy in digital networks. In an effort to downplay this leaked information, the NSA issued a statement claiming that it monitored just 1.6 percent of the 1,826 petabytes transmitted on a daily basis, mostly by collecting the twenty-nine petabytes sent via undersea cables. Of this data, supposedly only 0.025 percent is subjected to further processing, which would constitute merely 0.00004 percent of global data transmissions (National Security Agency 2013). If, however, all of the peer-to-peer services and video-streaming are weeded out from the total of worldwide traffic, 1.6 percent of the rest is anything but insignificant. If the storage process is further refined, if repeatedly visited sites are not repeatedly saved, and if images are ignored, then it would not be outlandish to suppose that this 1.6 percent of total traffic is enough to intercept every single email that is sent on a given day.[26] The NSA's program known as MonsterMind, which Snowden discussed in an interview with James Bamford, is being designed to identify and kill any suspected foreign cyber-attacks, such as distributed denial of service (DDoS) attacks, upon their arrival in the United States (Bamford 2014).

Nothing has yet to be leaked regarding the treatment of metadata, though sources such as the *Wall Street Journal* have reported that seventy-five percent of the metadata of all traffic in the United States and even eighty percent of all telephone conversations is being monitored (see Gorman and Valentino-DeVries 2013; Loewenstein 2014). Regarding mobile phones alone, the documents from Snowden's archive have revealed that five billion data records from several hundred million devices are being collected daily, on the basis of which conclusions can be drawn about the locations of their users (see Gellman and Soltani 2013). Thus it is no surprise that the NSA has been able, in the case of every suspect, to monitor up to three degrees of

---

26   In a legal testimony, the computer scientist Edward W. Felten made the following estimations: "Assuming that there are approximately 3 billion calls made every day in the United States, and also assuming conservatively that each call record takes approximately 50 bytes to store, the mass call tracking program generates approximately 140 gigabytes of data every day, or about 50 terabytes of data each year." This much data can be saved on a handful of spare hard drives. Felten's calculations also apply to the court order, mentioned above, that was issued to Verizon (2013).

separation; that is, for a suspect with one hundred contacts, the agency will identify not only these people but also the thousands of their potential contacts as well. Even if, in the future, this is to be reduced to two degrees of separation, the number of people under surveillance will remain massive (see Bauman et al. 2014, 125).

It is a matter of dispute to what extent the NSA's "secret systems of suspicionless surveillance," as the journalist Glenn Green-wald has called them, have been successful (2014, 8). Although it is unclear precisely how these systems function, it is just as unclear to what extent they have continued to be implemented despite the onslaught of public criticism and despite the recent UN resolution, promoted in large part by Germany and Brazil, that identifies the protection of privacy as a basic principle of democracy (see Human Rights Council 2014).[27] It is clear, however, that the capabilities of these systems depend on the fact that all traffic has to pass through nodes, where it can be intercepted. The sheer amount of data and the problem of storing it may have impeded the thirty thousand internal and sixty thousand external employees of the NSA from accessing desired information about terrorist activities, but the efforts employed to this end were systematic and deliberate violations of civil liberties and inter-national law (on the numbers cited here, see Greenwald 2014, 76). Although the surveillance conducted by the NSA was allegedly restricted to foreigners, this seems highly unlikely in light of the global network of data streams. In this regard, the NSA's most urgent need is thus not for more powerful surveillance tools but rather simply for greater storage capacity. This latter need will reportedly be fulfilled by the new Mission Data Repository, a gigantic facility in Utah designed to store up to twelve exabytes of

27 For the NSA report on this topic, which was commissioned by the American government, see Clarke et al. (2014).

information.[28] If we believe the numbers provided by journalists, there would be around two gigabytes for every person on earth.

Edward Snowden's revelations have raised many other issues that can only be touched upon here. They concern the self-perception of everyone who uses the Internet as a democratic citizen. They oscillate between the colonization of privacy and the new significance of the press. It is telling that Snowden's first anonymous message to Greenwald consisted of a request for him to use *Pretty Good Privacy* (*PGP*) encryption for his email exchanges, without which Snowden would not have been willing to send him any secret documents. This request, which Greenwald waited a month to satisfy, almost put an end to Snowden's whistleblowing before it began.[29]

The debate to be held about these open questions and long-neglected challenges should consider that the relation of the state to its citizens has changed dramatically since the arrival of the Internet (in conjunction with the "War on Terror"). Not only are citizens more transparent to the state but also, on account of WikiLeaks and whistleblowers like Snowden, the state is now to some extent more transparent to its people. In any case, it remains questionable to what extent this new relation is compatible with the classical models of political science.[30]

---

28   Twelve exabytes correspond to twelve thousand petabytes, twelve million terabytes, or twelve billion gigabytes. Four hundred terabytes is enough to save all of the books that have ever been written, while three hundred petabytes would suffice to store all the American telephone conversations that have taken place in a given year (see Hill 2013).

29   See Greenwald (2014, 10). For a thorough introduction to setting up PGP and for additional information about encryption, see http://ssd.eff.org/.

30   In his book on the NSA, Bernhard H. F. Taureck has described this situation as a "democracy of surveillance," because the NSA has increasingly come to take over the role of religion in the post-secular age. His essay demonstrates how certain constitutional and political-theoretical shifts in the structure of power have resulted in what he calls a "monitorcracy" (*Monitorkratie*). Its function is based on the fact that the knowledge held by intelligence services exceeds that of humanity "by a hundredfold" (2014, 10). It remains unclear where these numbers are from and whether

In a co-authored article titled "After Snowden: Rethinking the Impact of Surveillance," a group of political scientists and sociologists have discussed the leaks' significance to sociology and have pointed out the difficulties involved with formulating a new theoretical framework:

> Most perplexingly, perhaps, we seem to be engaging with phenomena that are organized neither horizontally, in the manner of an internationalized array of more or less self-determining and territorialized states, nor vertically in the manner of a hierarchy of higher and lower authorities. Relations, lines of flight, networks, integrations and dis-integrations, spatiotemporal contractions and accelerations, simultaneities, reversals of internality and externality, increasingly elusive boundaries between inclusion and exclusion, or legitimacy and illegitimacy: the increasing familiarity of these, and other similar notions, suggests a powerful need for new conceptual and analytical resources. (Bauman et al. 2014, 124).

The authors of this article have consciously sidestepped the current narratives of big-brother surveillance, which simply presume that new technologies serve to enable more precise surveillance. They have focused instead on the social process in which intelligence services have become independent political actors that set their own goals. What we are facing regarding the transformation of secret-service practices has thus become evident: There will be new interrelations that transcend national

humanity's knowledge—by which he presumably means the stored amount of all written texts—can even be sensibly compared with the information collected by the NSA. It rather seems as though a categorical error has been made, as a consequence of which Taureck fails to discuss the incursion of the digital and all of its effects. His argumentation, however in tune it might be with the current political situation, does not pertain to any of the specific practices of the NSA and neglects to distinguish, for instance, between data and metadata. Thus it is perhaps not surprising that he also never mentions encryption as a potential counter-strategy.

boundaries and in which certain roles have been redefined; partners will simultaneously act both for and against one another's ambitions; and problems concerning national juris- diction will arise if, for instance, the German Federal Intelligence Service requests data from the NSA that it is not legally permitted to collect on its own, and vice versa, while at the same time it comes to light that the NSA has been instrumentalizing its ostensible partners. Big data will not be stopped by national borders.

All of this has culminated, first, in a shift from "a high degree of certainty about a small amount of data to a high degree of uncertainty about a large amount of data" (Bauman et al. 2014, 125); second, in an act of collaboration—by means of the global propensity for people to share private information online—between those under surveillance and those con- ducting it; and, third, in the forms of subjectivity created by such activity, according to which everyone has become a suspect and social relations have been commodified. At the same time as intelligence services were gaining independence, the new relation between surveillance and privacy altered the sphere in which subjects develop. Their relations to other subjects have become valuable, marketable, and processable. Regimes of surveillance are thus accompanied by new manners of subjectivation (*Sub- jektivierungsweisen*), which are also subject to micro-decisions.

The End of the Internet

After Snowden, the Internet is no longer supposed to be what it once was. Yet this future is also being threatened by another side—or was rather always under threat. The *third* reason behind the intensity of the present debates is the fear that the World Wide Web could come to an end (see Riley and Scott 2009). To put it bluntly, if the abolition of net neutrality becomes the norm, future portions of the previously freely accessible Internet will no longer be accessible to the users of certain providers. In structural terms—to be blunt again—this would hardly be any different from the situation in China, where Google or YouTube are being blocked with the technical methods discussed above. The danger is thus that the Internet would no longer be identical for every user, because each user would be dependent on his or her contract, on the practices of the provider in question, or on government regulations and therefore only be able to accomplish certain goals. In the urgent words of Tim Berners-Lee: "If we, the Web's users, allow these and other trends to proceed unchecked, the Web could be broken into fragmented islands. We could lose the freedom to connect with whichever Web sites we want" (quoted from Whitney 2010).

In this light especially, Snowden's revelations gain even greater significance. The act of eavesdropping on land-line telephone conversations during the Cold War or the age-old technique of intelligence services opening letters did not jeopardize or cast doubt on these communications media (on tele-phone surveillance, see Rieger 2008). Yet the scope of online surveillance, in light of the fact that nearly all paths of com-munication run through servers and routers, casts doubt on the architecture of the Internet itself—or, as activist Sascha Lobo has put it: "The Internet is *kaputt*" (2014). Lobo admittedly presup-poses that a healthy Internet must necessarily be free, neutral, and open. The question remains, however, of how the opposite of a non-neutral, monitored, and closed Internet could or should be modeled.

In November of 2014, the White House released a YouTube video with a short speech by Barack Obama in which he acknowledged, with greater clarity than ever before, the issue of net neu-trality. Here he insisted that the FCC, an independent authority established in 1934 to regulate all transmissions of information, should establish rules to protect the unconditional neutrality of all data packets and should not impede the democratic and eco-nomic function of the "vibrant ecosystem of digital devices, apps, and platforms that fuel growth and expand opportunity." He went on to say, "As long as I am president, that is what I am fighting for" (White House 2014). The impetus behind Obama's plea was a decision reached in 2005 to treat providers as "information services," which are subject to fewer potential regulations, and not as "telecommunications services." Obama pointed out that this definition is obsolete and that providers should henceforth be understood as providers of telecommunications services that fulfill important functions in society and should thus be subject to greater scrutiny. According to the position held by Tim Wu, this means that telecommunication should be treated as a common good that serves the welfare of society and therefore should not be subordinated to private interests (see Scola 2014).

However noteworthy and important Obama's statements might be, given that they were the first comments to be issued by a government in favor of unconditional neutrality, they indicate all the more how important it is to think about net neutrality and surveillance in an integrated manner. For, however unconditional it might seem, the neutrality being promoted by the winner of the Nobel Peace Prize can, for simple legal reasons, not exist: Surveillance for purposes of law enforcement—and thus the use of hardware for purposes of network management—is codified in the law and more or less impervious to any debate. Under Obama's leadership, in fact, the authority of the NSA has been extended even further. Every single data record can fall under the NSA's control because decisions have to be made about their dissemination. To this end, every transmission has to be interrupted. This window of time is the habitat of the NSA; or, as Friedrich Kittler so perspicaciously remarked in 1986: "The NSA as the collapse of strategy and technology would be information itself" (Kittler 1986/2014). After Snowden, net neutrality can no longer be discussed in the same terms as it had been prior to his revelations.

Only a few days after Obama's statement, Republicans in the US Senate rejected a bill, known as the USA Freedom Act, that would have brought about large reforms to the NSA. Proposed by the Democratic government, this bill also enjoyed massive support from providers of digital services (see Ackerman 2014). The law would have limited the mass surveillance of metadata and greatly restricted the capacities of programs such as PRISM. Under the new provision, data would have admittedly continued to be collected by providers for a period of eighteen months, but the NSA only would have had access to this information if it were demonstrably useful for shedding light on or preventing acts of terrorism. And on December 4, 2014—only a few days after this vote had taken place—German Chancellor Angela Merkel announced at the *Digitising Europe Summit* that her government would support the establishment of a dual-class Internet. An Internet conducive to innovation, she said, "would be one in which there is a particular degree of security for special services. ... Therefore we need both: the free Internet and one with greater quality assurance for special services" (Merkel 2014). A free Internet, however, cannot be cut in half. Obama's speech, to the contrary, fulfilled its promise: In February of 2015, the FCC ruled in favor of net neutrality and released a set of constrictions for Internet service providers.

On account of the three reasons outlined above—increasing traffic volume, the possibilities of deep packet inspection, and the threatening inaccessibility of certain portions of the Internet—it has become clear that the debates over net neutrality and surveillance have been concerned with some of the greatest challenges being faced by today's digital cultures. All three of these reasons revolve around the role of micro-decisions. In order to understand what is at stake with them, at which times and places they are made, and how they can be used to promote certain interests, it will be necessary to delve more deeply into the technical architecture of data transmission. Or, as the computer scientist Agata Królikowski has noted: "The difference between observing and intervening, between blocking or delaying information and letting it pass through, simply comes down to a technical rule defined in the software, a rule that can be changed at any time" (2014, 158).

In order to introduce a different perspective, one that will serve as an apt transition to the next chapter, I would like to add that all of this can ultimately be reformulated in media-theoretical terms: The end-to-end principle potentially liberates communication and transmitted messages from surveillance by integrating interruptions into transmissions. During these interruptions, packets are admittedly processed before being forwarded, but this is done by means of a protocol for which the contents of the packets play no role at all. Transmissions do not follow any direct connection from A to B; rather, they are conveyed across a series of nodes and there are thus multiple possible connections. Because of this, these interruptions open up a timeframe for control. They are ambivalent to the extent that, while they admittedly serve to facilitate the unimpeded transportation of data, at the same time they represent the technical starting point for monitoring the traffic itself. From this perspective, net neutrality leads to a sort of unimpeded communication that can only be unimpeded to the extent that is stopped at every node of the network. Interruptions are inscribed into this sort of transmission. Between senders and receivers there are acts of interception. As my reading of Baran's network theory will show, it is precisely this point—describable as it is with the concepts of Claude Shannon's theory of communication—at which the significance and potential of communicating on digital networks can be negotiated beyond the implementation of micro-decisions. It is at this point, too, where the scope or dimension of micro-decisions is obscured by the phantasm of immediate, instantaneous transmission, a sort of transmission that allegedly requires no time and has always been determined in advance.

Flows Don't Burst: *Packet Switching* and the Instantaneity of Transmission

Although the extent of its influence has been a matter of debate, Paul Baran's 1964 article "On Distributed Communications Networks" can certainly be ranked among the central works of network theory to anticipate the development of the Internet. It was Baran's model of network architecture that gave rise to the structure of power in which micro-decisions are made on the basis of protocols. These technical conditions were accompanied by a new kind of network politics that has persisted to the present day. Thus was enabled the transition from targeted eavesdropping on individual connections to the diffuse surveillance of all connections, something which distinguishes the NSA's practices from those of earlier intelligence services. Equipped with the technical conditions for neutral transmissions that are based on decisions made at a network's nodes, Baran's model also contains the possibility of undoing this very neutrality.

The networks constructed later and the Internet itself admittedly differ in certain regards from Baran's machines, which only existed on paper. Instead of being distributed, his machines are scale-free; their individual nodes function as so-called hubs and they are able to process a vast number of connections.[31] It was not until the 1970s that some of Baran's ideas were adopted, in a roundabout way, to inform the construction of the Advanced Research Projects Agency Network (ARPANET) after the military and the telephone company AT&T had finally relented to make the transition from analog to digital transmission (see Brand 2003). Nevertheless, his text presented a novel approach to the technical aspects of time-critical transmission and to the micro-temporal synchronizations of information on networks.[32] It demonstrates with the utmost clarity that the success of networks necessarily depends on the micro-decisions that take place during the course of a transmission. Baran located these micro-decisions in the middle of the transmission process and also provided instructions as to how they are to be made. His model thus makes it possible to study the extent to which a given network theory of communication can be exposed to certain stipulations, economies, and contradictions. It also makes it possible to identify the theoretical and historical obstacles that have to be bypassed before anything can be implemented on a technical basis. Such obstacles are primarily time-critical in nature; they are theoretical and technical difficulties concerned with the proper times and micro-temporalities of networks and with the traditional desire to overcome temporal limitations—the desire, that is, for immediate transmission.

The paradoxical friction of transmissions being both limited by time and timeless is condensed into two metaphors: "bursting" and "flowing." The ideal operation of an electronic communications network is based on an uninterrupted,

31 See Barabási and Bonabeau (2003). In a discussion of scale-free networks in which many nodes have just a few connections while a few nodes have a great many, such as Internet sites like Facebook or Twitter, Martin Warnke (2013) has shown how the participation of all Web 2.0 users is subject to the terms and conditions of these large providers.

32 In various publications, Wolfgang Ernst has presented similar arguments about process-based and time-critical media. In his work, however, he seldom veers from theory to discuss specific technologies (see Ernst 2007).

continuous, and reliable flow of transmission. However, these transmissions can also be described as "bursts of information" (Abbate 2000, 19), as packet deliveries that, along their way, are constantly interrupted and lose time at every node. Such metaphors should not be confused with the technical details of frequencies and oscillations in cables or waves. They are rather part of a historical dynamic that, as I would like to show, arose out of the eighteenth-century sciences concerned with electricity and resurfaced anew in Baran's model. The following discussion is an attempt to understand the two modes of bursting and flowing as an articulation of a historically established approach to the temporal dimension of technical media. With respect to their politics, these two modes have opposing consequences, and therein lies their great significance to our perspective on today's networks: If everything were to be immediately connected to everything else, our potential courses of action would radically change—and certainly not in our favor. For if imme-diate communication were the case, all decisions would already be made in advance, there would be neither a time nor a place for interruptions, and thus there would be no way to change communication itself.

The argument offered in this chapter will thus be made on two different levels. On the one hand, I will investigate the technicity of Baran's model as regards its temporality and transmission capacity; on the other hand, I will relate all of this to the history of immediacy as it historically emerged from electricity research and reemerged in Baran's text. In seeking to combine—in a register that is quite different from that of the previous chapter—perspectives on engineering, technology, communication, and the history of science, I hope to delineate the underlying assumptions that have been made about temporality in these contexts. These assumptions will ultimately prove to be fun-damental to network politics, to the critique of such politics, and to our conception of media. It is in the matter of temporality that the significance of micro-decisions is most clear—as is the danger, however, that they will become hidden and invisible. My aim is to underscore what Jacques Derrida has called "coherence in contradiction," which "expresses the force of a desire" (2001, 352). In this case, the coherence of the contradiction between bursting and flowing is accompanied by the history of media. It is deeply embedded in the technological condition of the present. Such "coherence in contradiction" should not be thought of as a solution, for it is neither true nor false. It exerts, however, a sort of subliminal influence over the economy of Baran's text and its political imaginary. To follow these tracks means to pursue the phantasmatic dimension of technical media and their cultural influence.

In this sense, the following reflections can also be understood as approaches toward an archaeology of present-day technical infrastructures. They are meant to complement the present-oriented perspectives of the previous chapter (on media archae-ology in general, see Parikka 2012). Infrastructures are not simply tools or means of production. They are political because at their level micro-decisions are made about who can communicate and who cannot, what can be transmitted and what cannot, who is connected and who is kept apart. We should not simply leave these questions to engineers or even to politicians (whose judgment is based on the expertise of engineers). Perhaps, to some extent, we ourselves should become engineers or at least read what they have written and take apart what they have built.

In this respect, Baran treats the relations that people create through networks as neutral relations that are subjected to tech-nical processes. Who is connected with whom is, in his work, an insignificant issue, and the question of what it means to hinder social relations is never raised (this is surely because Baran's network was intended for government facilities and universities, where those who wished to communicate would have known each other in any case). It is of decisive importance, however, that the connections within the network were temporarily created for every transmission. Rather than being necessary, they were accidental. That means that the sociality potentially created through these connections has to be addressed on a new level. It cannot simply be superimposed by existing social relations but calls for the emergence of new relations.

Baran seeks a technical solution for a technical problem. Today, we see that both the problem and the solution cannot be separated from the social. Yet, as this technical network has spread to potentially every person on the planet, it has come to overlap with the social networks in which connections already exist and are perhaps necessary for maintaining the network itself. If technical and social networks converge—if, that is, technical possibilities of connecting come to overtake existing social connections, and new social connections are created by means of technical connections, as we are able to observe all around us today—then, unlike the situation in Baran's time, it will hardly still be possible to think about social relations in the absence of technical networks of communication. What had long been self-evident in the case of the postal system or the telephone gains a new dimension in light of the temporality, spatiality, and global availability of the Internet, a dimension whose political challenges should have been clear. Thus the first part of this essay had to be written in order to demonstrate here, in the second part, that the technical neutrality of the Internet—and the need to control distributions as well—depends first and foremost on something that is no longer possible today, namely the exclusion of the social. In this sense, thinking about the technical dimension of new media, even on the paths laid out by Friedrich Kittler (who preferred isolated PCs), necessarily implies thinking about the relations they create. This relational layer of sociality is based on the technicity of micro-decisions.

Threats of Destruction

The text under discussion is an abridged version of twelve longer works that Baran, an immigrant from Poland, had been contracted to write at the beginning of the 1960s by the RAND Corporation. His project in this matter was thus financed indirectly by the US Air Force. In his work for this think tank, which played a large role in the Cold War, Baran's task was to investigate how a communications network might be able to survive a nuclear attack and which forms of connectivity would be reasonable for the structure of this network to remain operational in the face of the most threatening of all threats.[33] That this network would one day be able to encompass the entire world—including Russia—was surely unthinkable at the time. When conducting this sort of work, it was typical to simulate war scenarios with the latest knowledge and technology. In addition to the military, Baran's paper for RAND also lists other parties interested in distributed networks: "[t]hose concerned with 'artificial intelligence,' . . . [t]hose concerned with communications within organisms and organizations, . . . [m]athematicians working with optimization of flow in networks, . . . [m]athematicians using dynamic programming to optimize incompletely understood and changing systems, . . . [and] [t]hose concerned with civilian common carrier telephone plant switching" (Baran 1964c, 2). It was for the same sort of specialists that Donald Davies would later orient the theoretical principles of the process known as packet switching.[34] The latter is a method for transmitting digitally coded data that divides such data into individual packets and transports them from one computer to another without there needing to be a direct connection between the packets. Through a network of multiple nodes, each of equal standing, every packet is sent along its own individual path and

33 In this case, "operational" meant that the system would be able to issue a command for a counterstrike.

34 Without any knowledge of Baran's work, Davies developed a similar process while working at the British National Physical Laboratory (see Davies 2001). Baran's model is not unique, but in its consideration of epistemological questions it is an especially revealing example of a development that was being made in various contexts at the time.

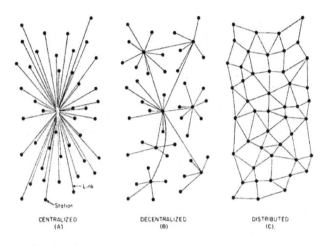

[Figure 2] Network Diagrams (Source: Baran 1964d, 1)

Baran distinguished three types of networks, the diagrams of which have become somewhat iconic in the Internet age: centralized, decentralized, and distributed (Figure 2). Centralized and decentralized networks are especially vulnerable because of their concentration on certain nodes at which all of the channels converge. As an alternative, Baran proposed a topology of distributed networks. Their essential feature is the "redundancy level" of their connections. It increases in conjunction with the digital coding of data because the packets can be reproduced at will. A centralized network, according to Baran, could be disabled with a simple strike against its central node, whereas a distributed network, with as many equal nodes as possible and just as many or more non-hierarchical connections, is nearly impossible to eliminate. For today's scale-free networks, however, it is the case that the removal of a few major hubs could cause considerable damage (see Barabási and Bonabeau 2003). Distributed networks nonetheless represent a solution by expanding and multiplying the potential targets of an attack on communications infrastructure. This network model requires communication to be entirely reconceptualized at the technical level, namely as constant interruptions that take place at every node and yet ultimately leave the impression that communication is based on direct connections.

Below I will concentrate neither on the developmental stages of this communications network, whose practical manifestations such as ARPANET and the Defense Advanced Research Projects Agency (DARPA), then directed by Ivan Sutherland, may or may not have been influenced much by Baran's work, nor on the social or political conditions in the 1960s that paved the way for distributed communications networks. As a number of studies have shown, Baran's text is steeped in the anxieties and political pressures of his time—anxieties and pressures for which applied scientists were hired to seek technical solutions.[35] The concept was neither patented nor kept secret in a deliberate attempt to provide the Soviet Union with the ability to construct a similarly secure communications network of its own. In the paradoxical logic of mutual assured destruction (MAD) the USSR's equally secure system would have meant greater security for the United States. Like so many theories of the time, Baran's approach was based on the threat of total annihilation and is thus characterized by an underlying apocalyptic tone—by an effort to confront the worst-case scenario. In order to destroy a distributed network, the enemy would have to strike at full capacity and eliminate *n of n* nodes (Figure 3). If only one node were disabled, there would still be a sufficient number of connections between all of the others. It is clear that such a design was motivated by the logic of escalation, according to which a series of nuclear attacks could potentially eliminate all of life on earth.

35 Peter Galison (2001) located the origin of this approach to networks in the operations research conducted by the Strategic Bombing Survey during the Second World War. He also described how this sort of knowledge was related to the shift of perspective from being one of the bombers to one of the potentially bombed. Christoph Engemann has more recently discussed these technical processes as a strategy for survival (Engemann 2010; see also Schröter 2004, 43; Gießmann 2009).

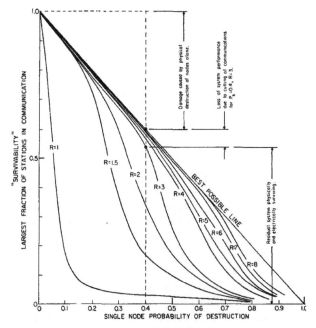

Fig. 4—Perfect switching in a distributed network: sensitivity to node destruction, 100 per cent of links operative.

[Figure 3] Node Destruction (Source: Baran 1964d, 2)

If this text is read in light of the context in which it was written, namely at one of most prominent think tanks during the Cold War, and if it is read as an attempt to prevent a preemptive nuclear strike, not only will the contrast become clear between the conflicts of that time and those of today. It will also become evident that the fundamentals of the Cold War threat and the reaction to it continue to live on today, even if the threats have changed or have largely been resolved. The historical place of Baran's text is characterized by the fact that, ever since his time, the transmission of communication, whether through postal or networked processes, has no longer been able to function in a frictionless manner. While it is true that remote communication has never been possible without control—"Control has existed from the beginning" (Galloway 2004, 142)—Baran's text represents an effort to control the distribution of information, a type of control that arose after the Second World War, was prompted by the computer, and was later on facilitated by Baran himself. It is impossible to understand our present circumstances without taking this form of control into consideration.

The Nodal Points of Decision-Making

The threat posed by the Cold War, which can be felt in every line of Baran's text, altered the definition of what communication means: It was no longer a matter of sending a message as quickly as possible from point A to point B. For the longest time, this had been the primary goal of many communication techniques (see Beniger 1986); within the framework of studying transmission delays, it also inspired the development of telegraphy and the physics behind it. The ideal type of this sort of communication creates direct connections between places, even though the technical architecture and economic benefits of networks had been known to be more advantageous than this approach since the time of optical telegraphy, which was established in France toward the end of the eighteenth century. The network approach to communication connects places through intermediate stations, relays, or nodes (see Siegert 1999). The network constructed by Claude Chappe on behalf of Napoleon was admittedly focused on Paris, but it covered as many transmitting stations as it could throughout the country. It was typical for the historical networks of optical and (later) electromagnetic telegraphy to be characterized by a central node at which multiple lines ran together and were distributed—as quickly as possible, as directly as possible, but vulnerable to targeted attacks threatening to disable the entire network in a single strike.

In Baran's perspective, the goal of secure transmission could only be achieved as something distinct from the goal of rapid communication. The network for secure transmission would thus have to be stabilized as "a new common-user system" (1964d, 5), one in which the number of nodes would be optimally coordinated with the number of connections. This would require, first of all, the use of a digital coding process that is protected against attacks by redundancy and can be automated; second, it would require the design of a communications infrastructure that has more lines or channels than are needed for normal operations. A network of this sort does not need to establish a direct connection between every node but rather relies on the stability of temporary connections. In the middle of the twentieth century, networking no longer implied the need of having to connect every destination with every other. According to Baran's calculation, a network of this sort could be made stable with a connectivity consisting of just three connections departing from every node. As a consequence it became more important to invest in distribution than in speed. In this regard, as Baran stressed, the factor of speed could be replaced by the factor of lower costs per message.

In Baran's model, every digitalized message is divided into standardized blocks of 1,024 bits and is assigned an identification number along with a header containing information about its address and sender. As is characteristic of the process of packet switching, each of these packets takes different paths and is reassembled at the destination on the basis of the information in the header. Although these packets were relatively small even for the circumstances of the time, their sheer mass played a special role. Simply put, Baran's method of packet switching re-determined, at every node, the optimal path that an incoming message should take to its destination by means of a continually updated timetable with the latest transmission times. Today, this process is governed by the protocol known as TCP/IP. In the case of every packet, an autonomous decision is made about which path it should take. If a given node happens to be disabled or overloaded, a sufficient number of other paths will still be available. Because the path to be taken is recalculated at every node, the packet has to be stored there briefly. The transmission is thus constantly interrupted.

Instead of creating as many direct and presumably fast connections as possible—that is, connections that are uninterrupted—the interruption itself was reconceived as that which ensures a network's security (in the sense of being indestructible): At every node, a packet can take a different path, one that is determined on an individual basis depending on the capacity of the network. Through the decisions that are made at such moments, the interruption of communication has become a precondition of its stability. To achieve this operational stability, every node must be able to survey the condition of the network and its fluctuating transmission times.

Baran's design implies that messages in postal, telegraphic, telephonic, or digital networks should not be sent directly from A to B but should rather be distributed in small stages between nodes, where they are to be stored temporarily. At the node, it is necessary to have information about the state of the network in order for a decision to be made about the subsequent route. To this end, the header is read. In addition to information about the destination and sender, the header contains a "handover number tag" that is updated at every node with information about the route that has been taken and about the duration of the transmission, as a measure of the respective condition of the network. This information assists in determining the further distribution of packets, which in a communications network of this sort would typically number in the thousands:

> The handover number is a tag in each message block set to zero upon initial transmission of the message block into the network. Every time the message block is passed on, the handover number is incremented. The handover number tag

on each message block indicates the length of time in the
network or path length. (1964d, 7)

On the one hand, this process serves to protect the communications system against attacks. On the other hand, however, it also serves to increase its productivity. Instead of sending information through a single channel, which could be either over- or underburdened, the overall load of the network can be evenly distributed by means of switching, which involves either storing a data packet a given node or sending it to an alternative node. Following the principle of what Peter Galison has called "constant vigilance against the re-creation of new centers" (2001, 20), today's technical variations of this process are nearly all based on decentralized communications infrastructures and protocols. The difference compared to Baran's model is that their architecture allows them to be scale-free (see Galloway 2004).

The act of interruption allows decisions to be made about the subsequent route of a packet. It is of time-critical importance. In the case of a telegraphic transmission, individual signals are sent in chronological order, and while they are admittedly not sent as a bit stream, they are nevertheless transmitted discretely. Accordingly, no message is present anywhere in the network in the form in which it was sent and in which it will be received after it has been reassembled. If a packet goes missing, it is reordered.[36] If a certain channel is occupied, the next shortest is chosen. What was novel about Baran's design was its combination of digitization, packets, and variable paths, which enabled a message to be fragmented into strictly delineated components that are redundant, that can each take its own path,

36   This process was later supplemented with so-called "time to live" (TTL). Because there is no predetermined path through the network, packets can occasionally take a long time hopping around between nodes. In order to reduce such wastes of time, the number of intermediate "hops" was limited. If a packet reaches its allotted number of hops before arriving at its destination, it is deleted (see Galloway 2004, 44).

and that can arrive in an arbitrary sequence.[37] The basis of this process was its introduction of constant interruptions. Although conceived as a technical solution at the time, these interruptions are now ostensibly being exploited in quite a new way.

The Immediacy of the Flow and the Interruption of Bursts

"On Distributed Communications Networks" subliminally evokes an instantaneity of transmission and an ideality of switching, both of which go hand in hand with their technical unfeasibility. It is in light of these notions that the role of micro-decisions emerges in Baran's model. It provides the toolkit for describing communication in terms of constant temporal interruptions, during which decisions are made about the further transmission of packets, and it situates the very stability of the network in these interruptions. In doing so, however, the model contradictorily relies on images that suggest presence and the continuity of transmission, both of which serve to conceal the necessity of decision-making.

My reading is aimed at the articulations of a particular tension—one that often comes to mind when thinking about communication or media—according to which communication or media erase the separation, overcome the delay, or negate the difference that they are predicated upon (see Peters 2000; Chang 1996). If the purpose of communication is to bring together that which is apart, it can, by achieving this, create the appearance of having eliminated the separation in question. The starting point of my reflections is that a medium of communication cannot or can only phantasmatically be immediate. Otherwise, it would bring the elements of the relation, between which it is

37   The noise of analog signals, which were used in the telephone transmissions
      of the time, become louder and louder with every node, which is why this
      method was then unsuitable for such an application.

mediating in a specific way and between which the uniting act of communication is taking place, into an unmediated relationship that would cause their separation and its mediation to disappear (see Sprenger 2012). As Michel Serres has stated, "A third exists before the second. A third exists before the others. . . . I have to go through the middle before reaching the end. There is always a mediate, a middle, and intermediary" (1992, 53). Media are admittedly the condition that enables two elements to be connected immediately with one another, for immediacy presupposes a relation between two or more elements. There is consequently no immediacy without media. Historically, the emphasis on the meaning of media is thus permeated by the dream of media-less immediacy.

This tension, which is observable in many manifestations throughout history, acquires particular significance through the fact that Baran's application is that of a network in which a decision has to be made about every distribution process, even those taking place between the shortest stages of transmission. In the final part of his treatise, Baran summarizes the goal of his project as follows: "An ideal electrical communications system can be defined as one that permits any person or machine to reliably and instantaneously communicate with any combination of other people or machines, anywhere, anytime, and at zero cost" (Baran 1964b, 1). Baran openly states that this illusionary goal is impossible to achieve. Actual communications systems, he notes, are always a compromise; they are never instantaneous and they cannot connect all communication partners simultaneously. As I hope to demonstrate, Baran excludes and includes this instantaneity at the same time. The danger in this is that the politics inscribed in the model threaten to become diffuse, even though they obey strictly defined rules.[38]

---

38 Matthew G. Kirschenbaum (2008) has observed the ideological feature of certain media theories to describe digital media as immaterial and ephemeral, whereas a close analysis of the material infrastructures of their objects reveals the opposite.

This ideal of an electrical or electronic communications network is defined by a constant, uninterrupted stream of transmission. In order to make the network appear stable, it should not capture the user's attention that decisions are constantly being made (and that they would later be a means of exerting power). The idea of "time-space-compression," which had a continued effect in discussions of "information superhighway" during the 1990s and is conjured up today as "real-time" transmission or connection, can also be found in the theoretical principles of Baran's design for a digital network. As mentioned above, such transmissions, which pass through a network and are never direct, can be described as "bursts of information" (Abbate 2000, 19)—as irregular collections of data packets that are characterized by phases of idleness and delay—and yet in the same stride he also evokes the image of regulated, omnipresent, uninterrupted, and continuous flow.[39]

Baran's text involves both of these metaphors with all of their implications and thus contributes to the tension outlined above. After all, that which flows cannot also burst, for to do so would be to interrupt the continuity of the river.[40] In a stream, continuous flowing can imply immediacy because, first, every flowing element follows uniformly and, second, this concatenated nature means that motion at one end of the river creates motion at the other. The image of the flow or of the "bit-stream" (Baran 1964a, 2) relies on the evidence that it takes place between A and B and everything sent flows the same path, while actually a network does not flow.[41] The network structure of today's communication channels and of their information streams is often understood

---

39   For a discussion of the "metaphysics of flux" and the "ontologies of flow," see Sutherland (2012).

40   On the metaphorical uses of the river throughout history, see the posthumously published study by Hans Blumenberg (2012).

41   On this matter it is also worth consulting another foundational text from the 1960s, namely Leonard Kleinrock's *Communication Nets* (1964), in which "flow" is modeled instead of "bursts" and a distinction is drawn between steady and unsteady flow.

as providing a direct connection between users and services or between two communication partners, even though there cannot be any direct connections on digital networks. The metaphor of the flow conceals the fact that, technically, what is taking place is quite the opposite. There is no stream in digital networks. That the metaphor suggests as much indicates that in this case—and in all of the metaphors associated with the Internet—the question of transmission and its technical details is not yet properly reflected. The economy of transmission, in which something can be in two places simultaneously, lends itself quite well to describing communication, which is supposed to be uninterrupted and frictionless. This was one of Baran's goals, but the technical means with which he achieved it happened to be the opposite of that which is implied by the metaphor of flowing.

In 1866, Werner von Siemens used a strikingly similar image in the context of describing electrical transmissions and the problem of their delay:

> This process can approximately be imagined as one in which a long, thin tube with elastic walls is pumped with air. Near the pump, the tube would be expanded by the elastic pressure of the incoming air every time the pump is deployed. This expansion would gradually decrease as the air reaches the open end of the tube, and the exit of the air from this end would only begin at full strength when the tube has taken on a conical shape. After the pump has been fully deployed, the tube would regain its normal diameter and the excess air would exit out of its far end. If the pump is pressed again before this emission is complete, the air would not appear at the far end intermittently; rather, the stream of air would no longer cease and it would flow constantly, though at varying speeds. (Siemens 1866, 37–38)

Whereas Siemens, in the last sentence quoted, implied a transition from bursts to flowing in the sense of oscillations and frequencies, which require time to begin, Baran would describe this shift on another level as an epistemological obstacle (I will discuss this in greater detail below). The "bursts of information" that arrive in a distributed network at arbitrary nodes are separate from one another. In their case, an absolute or constant speed is unthinkable, however much this might be implied by the metaphor of instantaneous flowing.

In pointing all of this out, it has not been my intention to dig up some sort of "repressed level" in Baran's work, to criticize his errors, or to claim that the dream of secure communications networks will remain a dream. The very fact that both metaphors are able to exist side by side is significant to the argumentation of this chapter. If Baran's text is read with an eye for such contradictory coherences, a number of unexpressed presuppositions come to light that ultimately culminate in the question of the instantaneity of transmission. Once the observation is made that Baran's design (even as a piece of pre-applicable theory) represents a historical shift in our understanding of communication, it gains even more significance in light of the historical issue of immediate and simultaneous transmission. Since the earliest experiments with electricity and telegraphy, this issue has influenced efforts to overcome distance for the sake of communication, and it persists today in sociological theories concerned with the consequences of such technical networks. Before further elucidating and contextualizing Baran's argumentation, I should perhaps first make a few remarks to illustrate the genealogy of the phantasm known as "real-time."

Electricity and Instantaneity

On a warm summer day in 1729, the dyer and physicist Stephen Gray suspended a brass wire on the property of his friend Granville Wheler's estate in Kent. When one end of the wire was touched with a rubbed tube of glass, small pieces of leaf brass began to dance like butterflies on the other end and settle on the wire (Figure 4). And thus from one end of the yard, without being able to see the outcome but rather relying on the sound of his friend's voice at the other end, Gray became convinced that he had generated an "Electrick Vertue"—attraction, electric power. Gray referred to the wires as "Lines of Communication" (1731, 27). In order for electricity to be able to communicate in Gray's sense, three elements are necessary: two entities attempting to communicate (one on each end), and whatever there might be between them. The sender and the receiver have to be apart from one another, for otherwise there would neither be a channel nor a connection. Communication requires distance; it requires a chasm, and connection requires separation. Not only does electricity surmount such distance; it also seems to do away with it altogether. It transmits by making the difference of time imperceptible and by dispelling space, by rendering both time and space immeasurable even though there is a piece of wire hanging through them.

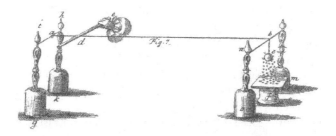

[Figure 4] Communication through Wires (Source: Doppelmayr 1744; Table 1)

Gray could not say whether electricity had a certain speed. As it seemed, it needed no mediation and no code; it was rather simply there, instantaneously and without any "perceivable difference" (Gray 1731, 28)—at both sides of the channel simultaneously. That which occurred at Gray's and Wheler's ends of the wire seemed to take place at the same time. An entire back yard can lie in between and soon an entire world, strewn with copper wire but requiring not a single minute, second, moment, or blink of delay. In the study of electricity, this *actio in distans*, which is caused by the sluggishness of our senses and the imprecision of measuring instruments, became extremely productive. With the advent of telegraphy it entered a broader discourse. At one point it was conceptualized as an "electric union" (van Rensselaer 1858, 5), even though it had long been obvious, in physical and technical terms, that every transmission requires time and that instantaneity cannot exist. Since the discovery of electrical conductivity in the 1730s, since the development of electromagnetic telegraphy in the 1830s, and since the subsequent implementation of a global electromagnetic communications network, electricity has been conceived to be instantaneous, its communication to be non-temporal, and its effects to be simultaneous.

The phantasmatic nature of this immediacy depends on the directness of its connections, which bring together two places, two devices, or two people but require no time to do so and are thus thought to abolish space. Although physics, then and now, has known this to be impossible, the idea is nevertheless maintained, in the sense of "coherence in contradiction," in the very contexts in which such impossibility happens to be obvious. Even the British physicist Charles Wheatstone, who had conducted the first successful experiments to measure the speed of electricity, attributed to it an instantaneity that negated the speed that he was attempting to investigate (see Wheatstone 1834). For in the end, an instantaneous transmission is at two places simultaneously; it is without time, space, or media—it is *im*mediate. There is more to this than simply the idea of unattainable instantaneity. The question bores deeply into the foundations of physics and is concerned with issues on its philosophical fringes such as causality, *actio in distans*, the ether, and ultimately the cohesion of the universe (see Hesse 1961). It has been discussed since antiquity, and even though it is not addressed directly in Baran's work, the profundity of the problem remains. The questions concerning the time-critical synchronization of distant events, which play a central role in Baran's studies, are not entirely absorbed by their technical and physical aspects. The tension between the metaphors of bursting and flowing derives from this history. Despite their differences, it draws a link between the early study of electricity and packet switching.

However often network theories tend to be influenced by such phantasms, they have featured just as prominently in sociological studies. In an extensive analysis of the synchronization practices of social time and flows, for instance, Manuel Castells has discussed networks and global interdependence in terms of the "annihilation of space and time by electronic means" (1998, 379). Castells describes real-time interaction as something that provides a venue for social connections—as something that allows locations to be shared simultaneously and actors to operate in the same space—even though there is in fact distance between them. On this basis, he asserts that the network society is "without reference to either past or future" (1998, 386). In the final pages of his book, Castells thus contradicts the painstakingly detailed argument that he had been making all along; just as he disregards the contingencies of globalization, at this point he also overlooks the effects of the convergence of technologies and social practices. In this regard, Castells's remarks are genealogically continuous with the popular discourses that, in line with the technical knowledge of the mid-nineteenth century, had established telegraphy as the instantaneous medium of a "world organism" (Kapp 1877, 100) and would recur in Marshall McLuhan's notion of "electric nowness" (McLuhan and Nevitt 1973, 2). The metaphor of the flow, the image of uninterruptedness, and instantaneous immediacy are common currency. As has already been indicated, they obscure the fact that a time and a place for interruptions are needed in order for decisions to be made.

Perfect Switching

The aim of the process outlined above is to balance out the load throughout the network. Its result is the elimination of instantaneity (*De-Instantanisierung*). When speed is no longer the primary goal, the idea of instantaneous transmission loses some of its appeal and is no longer favored as a technical solution. The fact that in Baran's text instantaneity nevertheless resurfaces as a discursive effect lies in the sort of economy that informs his idea of "perfect switching." This ideal form of communication is related to the information that the network possesses about its own condition as well as to the speed at which this information is transmitted.[42] Perfect switching thus makes it clear how the phantasm of instantaneity intervenes in the politics of networks.

Baran described the advantages of his process by drawing an analogy to a postman sorting the mail in the middle of the United States. In a "store-and-forward system," which he also refers to as "message switching" and in which entire messages are forwarded at every station, the postman will receive messages "simultaneously" from San Francisco, even though they had been sent at different times (Baran 1964d, 7). By comparing the transit times recorded on their postage stamps, he can then determine, assuming that the channel of communication is bidirectional, the best route for the letters or packages at his office that need to be sent in the opposite direction (that is, *to* San Francisco): "Each

---

42   In this sense, the distributed network is comparable to the "ordinary whale" that Hermann von Helmholtz mentions while describing the synchronization problems associated with the slow speed of nervous systems: "Happily the distances are short which have to be traversed by our sensuous perceptions before they reach the brain, otherwise our self-consciousness would lag far behind the present, and even behind the perceptions of sound . . . With an ordinary whale the case is perhaps more dubious; for in all probability the animal does not feel a wound near its tail until a second after it has been inflicted, and requires another second to send the command to the tail to defend itself" (1853, 325).

letter carries an implicit indication of its length of transmission path" (Baran 1964d, 7).

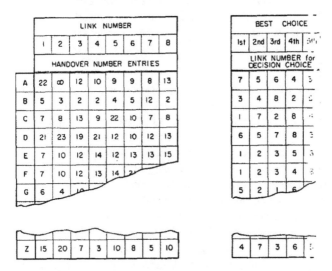

	LINK NUMBER							
	1	2	3	4	5	6	7	8
	HANDOVER NUMBER ENTRIES							
A	22	∞	12	10	9	9	8	13
B	5	3	2	2	4	5	12	2
C	7	8	13	9	22	10	7	8
D	21	23	19	21	12	10	12	13
E	7	10	12	14	12	13	13	15
F	7	10	12	13	14	2		
G	6	4						
Z	15	20	7	3	10	8	5	10

BEST CHOICE				
1st	2nd	3rd	4th	5th
LINK NUMBER for DECISION CHOICE				
7	5	6	4	3
3	4	8	2	2
1	7	2	8	4
6	5	7	8	3
1	2	3	5	5
1	2	3	4	8
5	2	1	6	
4	7	3	6	5

[Figure 5] Handover Number Table (Source: Baran 1964d, 7)

What is decisive in this is that the postman can extract information about the best route simply by looking at the stamped date of dispatch, which accompanies each piece of mail just as a handover number tag is meant to accompany every data packet (Figure 5). The message carries information about its own transmission, whether on its stamp or in its header. In their sheer number, the values on these "tags" indicate the amount of time needed to traverse from node to node up the point in question and thus provide information about the current state of the network and its workload. This information is tabulated and made available to be reviewed at every node. Thus it is possible to determine for each packet the optimal channel that it ought to take next—a channel into a future that has been extrapolated from data provided by the past. Initially, all of the entries on Baran's "handover number table" are given a high value, which is changed accordingly after the arrival of the next message. The system is able to learn, adapt itself, and constantly update its own status without the need for a center where all of this information is gathered. Because distributed networks lack such a center, every node has its own image of the overall network, that is, its own table. But what is the temporal component of this image?

Executed at every node (including those of centralized networks), switching is the process of transferring a message from one channel to another in order to bring it closer to its destination with the help of the information in the table. According to Baran, traditional switching does not create possibilities for redundancy because it provides only one route instead of multiple to choose from. Starting from a central node allows for few possible ways of reaching a destination. In a network based on Baran's model, a direct consequence of this process is the demand for increased computing and memory capacity at the nodes, a demand that happened to be met by steady improvements in micro-computing. In 1969, a comparable network with seven nodes was constructed in the western United States, namely ARPANET, from which the Internet would originate.[43]

Perfect switching, for which Baran had high hopes, designates a routing process that is "able to find 'best' surviving paths in a heavily damaged network" (Baran 1964c, 1). In undamaged networks, perfect switching is the ideal selection of routes. It is thus closely associated with the assumption of instantaneous transmission and real-time: "[T]he shortest instantaneously available path through the network should be found with the expectation that the status of the network will be rapidly changing" (Baran 1964d, 6). Its precise goal is to avoid direct connections in favor of there being multiple routes, out of which

---

43   In his book *Die Verbundenheit der Dinge* ("The Connectedness of Things"), Sebastian Gießmann traces the origin of ARPANET back to Baran's network ideas (2014, 355–56).

the optimal one can be selected at any given point on the basis of the traffic that is burdening the surrounding nodes: "Perfect switching provides an upper bound of expected system performance for a gridded network; the diversity of assignment case provides a lower bound" (Baran 1964d, 4). However, for perfect switching to work (and this applies to "imperfect switching" as well), each node must possess information about the status of the network.

Synchronization processes are therefore necessary to make information available to each node about its specific status within the network. By equipping packets with information about their transmission times and using this information to update his network, however, Baran was faced with the fundamental physical problems of relativity and synchronization (see Galison 2003): The transmission of this information, which is supposed to be used simultaneously to ascertain the present state of the nodes, itself requires time. As Sebastian Gießmann has shown (2009, 245), the "disparate time regime" of this transmission is time-critical to the extent that the status of the network and the workload of the nodes change along with the economizing optimizations that take place during the transmission itself. Every packet carries a piece of this information, and as a mass they provide the node with the data necessary to form a serviceable map. However, because the information about transmission times is obsolete at the moment that it arrives at a given node (because the transmission of this information about transmission times itself requires time), it can only ever provide an image of the past. In the time needed for a packet to move from one node to another, which might have seemed to be the optimal next step at the moment the packet was sent, the node in question could already be occupied with other packets. In all of its perfection, perfect switching requires exact information about the present state of affairs; such real-time information, however, is in fact technically impossible to attain. This relativistic shift, which undermines any requirement for real-time data, is both technically and physically insoluble because no signal is instantaneous and distant effects cannot be achieved immediately. Real-time can only mean that signals are arriving at the speed in which they can be processed as quickly as possible: in time rather than real-time. Real-time always takes place between two points in time and is therefore not instantaneous. At this point, again, the tension comes into play that is inherent to communication in its electrical or electronic implementation.

The network has neither knowledge nor control of its present condition but rather only of those past conditions from which an optimal distribution of packets was extrapolated for the future. The process of synchronization reduces time-critically differing temporalities to a single denominator without ever being able to achieve real-time or simultaneity. Synchronization is the coordination of multiple levels of time; it is an attempt to harmonize various technical orders in an effort to operate with differences.[44] Its goal is not (and cannot be) to achieve concurrence but rather to determine the limits between which the desired event can take place, and in this case the desired event is successful transmission. Two processes or events are therefore synchronous if they do not exceed the interval of time that is required for a technical process to run. In other words, every act of synchronization contains a remnant of time-bound transmission that cannot be simultaneous; at best, it can be timely enough that the delay does not affect the technical

44   One of Baran's footnotes, which concerns the importance of the "velocity of propagation over long links," is thus especially telling in this regard: "3000 miles at ≈ 150,000 miles/sec ≈ 50 msec transmission time, T. 1024-bit message at 1,500,000 bits/sec ≈ 2/3 msec message time, M. Therefore, T >> M" (1964d, 6). In these formulas, the entire model is defined as a synchronization process, and this is because communication can only succeed if the time of transmission and that of processing are coordinated with one another. The standardization of data into quickly processable blocks of information should thus be understood as a response to the problem of synchronization.

process in question.[45] For switching to be technically successful, the information about the workload of the nodes only has to be timely enough to enable the decision for an alternative route. As such, synchronization is not the production of real-time (*Echtzeit*) but rather of timeliness (*Rechtzeitigkeit*), and this is because it is dependent on limits (on the notion of "timeliness," see Rohrhuber 2009 and Pias 2009). This timeliness, with which imperfect switching can operate smoothly, is achieved by complying with certain limits; it is not the sort of metaphysical exactness implied by the term "simultaneity." Baran referred to his process as "hot-potato routing" because the packets were to be passed along as quickly as possible from node to node like hot potatoes (so as to avoid congestion and burnt hands): "Each message is regarded as a 'hot potato,' and rather than hold the hot potato, the node tosses the message to its neighbor who will now try to get rid of the message" (Baran 1964d, 7). To stick with this metaphor, synchronization operates with the time that occurs between catching a hot potato and the onset of pain.

If the perfect path were instantaneously available, the information at the respective node would have to be perfectly up to date, which it can never be. The table would have to indicate the condition of all the nodes simultaneously in order for perfect switching to be guaranteed, which would in turn mean that the information would be everywhere at the same time. A flow or an uninterrupted stream of information would be necessary where there happens only to be bursts. Perfect switching implies the instantaneity of switching, which presupposes the instantaneous transmission of necessary information. In such a case, the network would be present to itself. This cascade would end in a self-presence that is characteristic of the medium of voice, which for the speaker is no longer a medium because it does not have to be transmitted to him or her: "Everything had

---

45   TCP/IP accounts for such delays in advance by having a built-in tolerance for runtime errors and deviations. Difference is thus inherent to the protocol.

to be estimated instantaneously, if voice was to be transmitted, as voice is intolerant to delay" (Baran 2002, 5). There is no room for interruption in the self-presence of voice (see Derrida 2011). Yet interruptions are there. The network, which is stabilized by interruptions, should collapse.

The Disconnection of Connection

As we experience whenever we are online, however, the network has not collapsed. Despite the delays in question, it continues to operate. Thus, immediacy and interruption are not significant at the level of daily experience. Baran drew attention to the fact that the form of transmission designed by him can appear to be direct and electrically instantaneous even though it requires intermediate steps:

> The network user who has called up a "virtual connection" to an end station and has transmitted messages across the United States in a fraction of a second might also view the system as a black box providing an apparent circuit connection across the country. (1964d, 6)

As Baran noted, a circuit connection takes place in "real-time" because there are no nodes but rather a direct connection between A and B. The transmission appears to occur in "real-time" because electricity is presumed to be instantaneous and there are no nodes to break the connection. To a user who is receiving data, listening to a voice on the telephone, or even responding to this voice, transmissions sent by means of packet switching may appear to be occurring in "quasi-real-time" (Baran 1964d, 6), as though they have been produced with the circuit switching used to make telegraphic direct connections. For the user it can seem as though there is no pause, delay, or separation and as though he or she is interacting in a conversation or surfing on a website in a Platonistically present manner. Although the user's communication partner is in a distant location, the

seemingly simultaneous connection provided by the network
leaves the impression that this distance does not exist.

Baran's epistemological reflections on this connection concern
the precarious status of media, which, from a theoretical perspective, can be made "readable, audible, visible, and perceptible,
all the while exhibiting the tendency to extinguish themselves
and their constitutive participation in these sensualities and thus,
as it were, to become imperceptible, anaesthetic" (Engell and Vogl
1999, 10). With all the openness expected of an engineer, Baran
summarized the disconnection of the user through the invisibility
of the medium as follows:

> This choice meant that there would be no physical real-time
> connection between the transmitting and receiving end. But,
> I felt that would be OK if the transmission data rate was high
> enough, the user would be fooled by the illusion that a real-
> time connection existed. (Baran 2002, 4)

Baran's idea is in tune with a thought expressed by Marshall
McLuhan, namely that media are invisible to their users: "Indeed,
it is only too typical that the 'content' of any medium blinds us
to the character of the medium" (McLuhan 1964, 9). This thesis
about the disappearance of media, which has become well
established in media studies (see Mersch 2004 and Jäger 2004)
and has been referred to as "aesthetic neutrality" (Krämer 2003,
81), is expressed by Baran within the framework of a technically
conceived model. The illusion of the user is the flipside of the
technical knowledge of the engineer. Illusion is flow, transmission
is burst—and both are entwined on the imaginary level of the
text.

Pragmatically—and as far as everyday life is concerned—this
illusion may be inconsequential. Whoever is communicating over
a network is not meant to be aware of the fact a series of imperceptible decisions is being made about the data packets that constitute his or her communication. This has no implication for our
phenomenological perspective, for our social interactions, and

for any theory of communication that is only concerned with the success of communication:

> On the contrary, the other person whom I am able to call is "present" to me in an emphatic and immediately relevant way. He is "simultaneous" with me but not in the sense that he is doing this or that at the same time as I am doing such things. Rather, he is "simultaneous" with me to the extent that the meaningfulness of his activity can be expressed to me at any given time—and vice versa. (Konitzer 2005, 196)

Even if disruptions and interruptions might hinder our ability to understand someone on the telephone or to reload a website, we are still able to relate to one another in a convincing manner. For successful communication, it is sufficient to know that the other is quasi-present.

In this regard, that which happens to play no role in daily life is in fact all the more relevant both politically and in terms of media theory. The place of transmission evoked by Baran—along with its delays, its difference, and the interruptions during which decisions are made—are issues of immediate concern to the "fooled" user: To be able to interrupt communication is to possess power. To be able to do this without being observed, moreover, is to exert an invisible sort of power. Such power will threaten to become unassailable if transmissions are presumed to be truly instantaneous. The illusion of connection cited by Baran will inhibit the very network politics of interruption that his model introduced, as will any media theory that claims transmissions to be instantaneous.[46] By following such paths, we will neither be able to confront the challenge of government-sponsored surveillance nor that of net neutrality, even though Baran's text is part of their origin.

---

46 See, for instance, McLuhan and Nevitt (1973) and Virilio (2000). For a more comprehensive discussion of this issue, see Sprenger (2012).

Conclusion: Toward a Network Politics of Interruption

The idea of controlling digital networks with decisions, as demonstrated by Baran's model, was conceived to solve a specific technical problem. It emerged at a particular historical moment and subsequently served various purposes. Micro-decisions are neither inherently good nor inherently bad. For the operations of a digital network, however, they are unavoidable. In order to maintain the possibility of altering the scope of such decisions, it is therefore important to protect them from being appropriated and to be aware of the historical situations in which they became plausible. If we could succeed in developing a sort of network politics that combines this historical perspective with what is happening in the present—that is, if network politics were to be aware of the history of the Internet's architecture in relation to the current debates about net neutrality and surveillance, then perhaps returning to the beginnings would provide us with new insight into possible futures. It could come to light that decisions, though necessary, do not necessarily have to be made always and already in advance of a given transmission; that every transmission may indeed be an exertion of power, but networks allow for such power to be distributed; and that, while it may be impossible for traffic to exist without control, the traffic always precedes the control in question. A network politics of this sort could, in response to the deluge of connections that we face on a daily basis, fight to preserve a space for disconnections in life and it could furthermore do much to draw a firm line between control and surveillance.

By way of conclusion, I should therefore take another look at the connections and disconnections that result from these decisions. Over the course of this essay, I have focused on some of the times and places at which the conditions for micro-decisions have been created by means of the protocological principle. To these occasions could be added the establishment of the X.25 protocol for telephone networks, the development of ARPANET and the French network known as Cyclades, the many stages of TCP/IP's implementation, and the present development of the so-called Internet of things, which makes our environment predictable. What is common to these examples is that there are not only places and times at which the standards of micro-decisions have been institutionally determined; what is more, they themselves generate places in the network and obey a temporality of their own. Decisions are made at these places in order for things to proceed independently within a specific temporality. These places and times lend themselves to a media-archaeological per-spective that, in a strict sense, should not be separated from the network-political implications of its findings.

Given the depth of their effects, the modes of operating technical networks and their media should be understood above all in terms of the way that they make use of synchronization to process differences. Transmissions of digital data in distributed or scale-free networks—from browsing to high-frequency trading and the Internet of things—are so effective precisely because they are constantly interrupted (while admittedly operating at the highest possible speed). Taking the history of such networks into account, one could even assume that they are technically

possible only because they are not and cannot be instantaneous.
A continuous flow would wash away all differences and thus
also do away with the separation or disconnection that media
presuppose and require. The concealment or obscuration of
interruption, for which evidence can be found in a variety of historical contexts, has technical and theoretical consequences as
well as political effects. If transmission is conceived in terms of
overcoming distance, as in Castells's notion of the "annihilation
of space and time by electronic means" (1998, 379), then we will
lose sight, like Baran's deceived user, of the operational modes of
digital networks and thus also lose sight of their politics of connection and disconnection. What appears to reach our screens
as a continuous flow is in fact a series of bursts composed of
information. Decisions are made about every burst, and these
decisions have political implications. They determine who can
be connected and who is disconnected. If data were in fact
flowing, transmission would be instantaneous; there would be
no decisions because there would be neither a time nor a place
for them. They would then always be made in advance and
could not be changed. In other words: Theories of immediacy
are instructions on how to be powerless. By obscuring the times
and places of such decision-making, we would be in danger of
neglecting the possibility of discussing the processes with which
technical standards and modes of distribution have been transformed and thus shaped by interrupted streams—the processes
that determine who is connected with whom and who is disconnected from whom.

Baran's economy of communication is ultimately not aimed at
avoiding the high costs of unused channels or nodes caused by
pauses and idle moments between transmissions. The problem
of overloaded nodes did not exist at the beginning of the
1960s. In light of the excess capacity at the time, neutrality and
prioritization were thus not things that would have had to be
considered. It could therefore hardly have seemed like a political
act of the highest order to integrate, at the technical level, a sort

of neutrality that was at first simply meant to serve the compatibility of hardware, applications, and content. Today, however, these issues are far more portentous: The use of prioritization to manage overloaded networks is no longer simply a technical problem; it has also become a social and political problem of growing virulence. In turn, it has thereby also become clear that the technical solutions of the 1960s, which were discovered under different circumstances, are still exerting effects under our present conditions. Accordingly, Baran's model provided the framework that gave rise to the present necessity of bandwidth management and the corresponding political status of micro-decisions. Though under different conditions, they have been inscribed in the network architecture since 1964 and they have been political decisions the entire time. This is so even if, in 1964, they were made without discrimination and could therefore appear to be democratic until the network became overloaded. Before that point, that is, decisions still had to be made but they did not prioritize anyone over anyone else. The success of the Internet since the 1990s is not only politicized in the trivial sense that it serves as forum for expressing opinions, intervening, and organizing. Through this success, its infrastructure has rather become the global foundation for social connections; sociality and technology have thus become so tightly intertwined that it is impossible to say which preceded the other. If this infrastructure were to change, or even if its functionality were called into question, then there would be ineluctable repercussions for the constitution of the social.

These observations have a series of consequences for a network politics of interruption and for the opposition against the decisions in question. As it is, the decision-making process cannot be denied; to do so would be to deny the very thing about which decisions are being made: the transmission of data in digital networks. That decisions are being made cannot be treated as a matter of negotiation; to do this would be to dismantle the foundation of the very object under negotiation. The difficulty of finding an oppositional perspective lies in the fact that these decisions enable that which we are fighting for. In this situation, it is thus difficult to adopt an unambiguous position. There is instead a discursive strategy at our disposal, one that has been endorsed by the Chaos Computer Club and the *Electronic Frontier Foundation*, that can be deployed to give users a voice in digital cultures and offers them some means of self-defense: On the one hand, this strategy involves the expansion of social debates and the demand for providers to make their procedures transparent; on the other hand, it involves teaching individuals about encryption and technical processes in order to oppose the enforced transparency with anonymous intransparency.

This pragmatism accepts the technical circumstances in order to improve them and to oppose the loss of control that the blogger Michael Seemann has described as an effect of digital connectivity (see Seemann 2015). On another level, it employs the sort of analysis that Alexander Galloway and Eugene Thacker executed in their book *The Exploit*.[47] Its goal is to investigate the protocols and standards of networks that regulate what happens with delayed data and thus determine who can be connected with whom and what can or cannot be said and done.[48] Galloway

---

47 See Galloway and Thacker (2007). Even in Galloway's work, however, there is mention of instantaneous transmission: "Just as Marx descended into the internal structure of the commodity to interpret its material workings within the context of production at large, I must descend instead into the distributed networks, the programming languages, the computer protocols, and other digital technologies that have transformed twenty-first-century production into a vital mass of immaterial flows and instantaneous transactions" (Galloway 2004, 20). Here, too, Derrida's idea of "coherence in contradiction" is evident, in that Galloway demonstrates the opposite of what his metaphor implies.

48 Under digital conditions, discourse analysis could be applied—and I understand that this new orientation is obvious by now—not only at the level of the archive but also at the level of micro-decisions, protocols, or algorithms. Like traditional instruments of power, they likewise determine what can be said and seen. Perhaps the next step would be to reformulate the methods of discourse analysis and media archaeology at this level in order to keep up with technical developments. The goal, in other words, would be to analyze

and Thacker's intention is to leverage the prevailing powers: "Yet within protocological networks, political acts generally happen not by shifting power from one place to another but by exploiting power differentials already existing in the system" (Galloway 2004, 81). As hackers understand the word, an "exploit" is a vulnerable element in a system that allows the powers at play to be used to new ends. In order to take advantage of such opportunities and exploit the immanent dynamics of a given system—a tactic, as it were, that is indirect and yet responds to the moment—it is necessary to have a deep understanding of the structure that one wishes to change. Only with a firm command of the rules will we be able to undermine them, affirm them, or rewrite them to our liking. Such attempts appear helpless in their effort to maintain a type of sovereignty that binds control to a subject. Who should know who has access to which data? The conditions of such sovereignty have changed so radically that it is by now high time to reexamine their technological underpinnings. No one has control in digital networks, and this is because digital networks are themselves nothing if not the decision-bound control of their distribution.

A politics of this sort thus ought to begin at the level of micro-decisions and thus at the places and times of decision-making. As interruptions, they are central to understanding the structure of networks. They have locations because they are nodes in the network that break up direct connections; they are temporal because time is what interruptions require—always more than one would like, and yet this duration is a precondition for the network's very possibility. Interruptions are what Edward Snowden referred to as "one-stop-shops" (Mestmacher-Steiner 2014): At one step, in a short amount of time, and at a single place, they allow for a variety of things to be accomplished. It is not necessary to monitor every terminal; a single node will

what it is that networks, by means of connections and disconnections, have allowed or disallowed to be said.

suffice. An alternative network politics can organize itself around these interruptions, delays, and differences. Beyond looking for exploits, which Galloway and Thacker have defined as vulnerabilities within systems of power that are capable of being modulated, an alternative network politics should not only make interruption its mode of operation but should also understand interruption as communication. In every digital network, interruption is the primary mode of operation. Because of interruptions, transmissions can be made.

From this point, as I would like to note in closing, alternative forms of organization should be sought that no longer aim to produce immediate connections but are rather founded on interruptions, which are inevitable in any case, and on the accidence of connections. A collective of this sort would have to understand its own disconnections—the interruption of its connections—not as a threat to be combated but rather as an advantage over those that require connectivity only to lose it upon its interruption. Connections are created, but disconnections or separations are as well. Interruptions could lead to an organizational mode of disorganization. An "organization of the organizationless," as the social theorist Rodrigo Nunes (2014) has promoted, could in this sense also be understood as an affirmation of interruption that is aware of the fact that decisions are being made about its connections, that control is inevitable, but that control can be undermined. Parallel to this, new network architectures, such as Recursive InterNetwork Architecture (RINA), could introduce new possibilities for changing the controversial aspects of today's networks while remaining faithful to their underlying principles (see Day 2010).

In other words, the difference between control and surveillance in digital networks in the post-Snowden era has become clearer, as has the need to control this control and to circumvent surveillance. The prerequisite for this course of action is the technically codified condition that there can be no central authority for making decisions but rather only local applications of protocological modes of power at every node (see Galloway 2004, 82). This architecture allots a precarious status to the political in networks: To change the protocol is to meddle with the preconditions of its own activity. To control the application of the protocol can only be achieved with additional protocols. And to disclose micro-decisions as decisions, to write their history, and to recognize their places and times may admittedly be to criticize them, but this in itself changes nothing. In this way, however, the detailed work of network politics, as has been exemplified in the public debates over net neutrality, would certainly be placed on a firmer foundation.

This essay has analyzed the "cultural techniques of synchro-nization" (see Kassung and Macho 2012) that ensure the timely nature of communication and are thus central to an archaeology of real-time and to a genealogy of its phantasms. To the extent that they are entwined, they demonstrate that the history of media and the history of immediacy are closely associated with one another. Moreover, they also demonstrate how deeply the micro-decisions of transmission have become embedded in the "technological condition" (Hörl 2011) of the present. Herein lies the significance of future developments in net neutrality and of the political consequences of the NSA revelations. Despite our apparent obsession with the present, history lessons are nec-essary to ensure that we will continue to have a voice in digital cultures.

In short, the question is whether we want to live in a world that appears to flow because every decision has already been made—in an opaque manner, given that we will not have any access to the background where constant interruptions and decisions are indeed taking place—or whether we want to live in a world that will never be present to itself and in which, though there will be no immediacy, every decision at every node can be altered and remain open to new possibilities. We cannot avoid this ques-tion because we are already caught in its net (so to speak). We can, however, use the power of interruption to our own ends.

The potential emergency of their being a continuous, uninterrupted period of decision-making can be diverted if decisions
could continue to be identified, despite their massive number, on
an individual basis. This could remain possible so long as their
times and places are known. If decision-making were to become
normal, if it were to become simply a condition of everyday life,
then, as Giorgio Agamben has suggested (2014), the idea of crisis,
which has always designated a moment of decision-making,
would lose its temporal index and become a common state of
affairs. It would be frictionless and devoid of interruption. In this
sense, digital cultures can be cultures of crises (see Chun 2011).

Perhaps, however, an even greater challenge is looming in a
different place altogether: Micro-decisions are made by machines
both for and about other machines. Although we might still be
able to identify individual decisions, we will always be too late to
the scene, because their sheer number and speed exceeds our
capacities. If machines communicate only with machines and
people are mere accessories at the ends of the nodes, if the interests of power continue to be served by newer and more precise
machines, and if decisions no longer have decision-makers, then
the actual task before us will have shifted. It could then be the
case that our traditional description languages, our concepts of
humans and machines, of creation, work, and activity will have
become too imprecise to comprehend what is happening and
who is supervising whom. Perhaps they are no longer sufficient
for understanding machines that neither render human beings
superfluous nor were designed according to our model. Confronted with the question of what control and surveillance might
mean in this situation, I would like to bring my essay to a close.

Acknowledgments

An earlier version of the second part of this essay was presented in 2012 at the conference *Network Archaeology*, which was hosted by Miami University in Ohio. I am grateful to the organizers of that event, Cris Cheek and Nicole Starosielski, and for our fruitful discussions. Sebastian Gießmann, Till Heilmann, and Christoph Engemann, who each read drafts of this text with generous care, have helped me avoid a number of pitfalls. Moreover, I am indebted to Götz Bachmann, Paul Feigelfeld, Yuk Hui, and Scott Lash for allowing me to present a later stage of this work at the conference *Data & Technics*, which took place in 2014 at the Leuphana University in Lüneburg. Without the steady encouragment of Erich Hörl and Götz Bachmann, who urged me to focus on the political aspects of my ideas, this book never would have taken its present shape.

Thanks are also due to my colleagues at the Digital Cultures Research Lab, and especially to the editors of the book series *Digital Cultures*. Without the involvement and support of the meson press—and in particular its representatives Marcus Burkhardt and Andreas Kirchner—this book never would have been possible. Valentine Pakis's careful and precise translation has made it available to a wider audience, for which I am thankful, and Sebastian Lehr deserves my gratitude for looking at my work with an outsider's perspective, identifying certain inconsistencies in my thinking, and helping me to refine my arguments. It is to Regina Wuzella, however, that I offer my warmest expression of appreciation.

Works Cited

Abbate, Janet. 2000. *Inventing the Internet*. Cambridge, MA: MIT Press.

Ackerman, Spencer. 2014. "Senate Republicans Block USA Freedom Act Surveillance Reform Bill." Accessed January 19, 2015. http://www.theguardian.com/us-news/2014/nov/18/usa-freedom-act-republicans-block-bill.

Agamben, Giorgio. 2014. "For a Theory of Destituent Power." *Chronos* 10 (February 2014). Accessed January 19, 2015. http://www.chronosmag.eu/index.php/g-agamben-for-a-theory-of-destituent-power.html.

Apple 2015. "We've Built Privacy into the Things You Use Every Day." Accessed January 19, 2015. http://www.apple.com/privacy/privacy-built-in/.

Bamford, James. 1982. *The Puzzle Palace: A Report on America's Most Secret Agency*. Boston: Houghton Mifflin.

———. 2008. *The Shadow Factory: The Ultra-Secret NSA from 9/11 to the Eavesdropping on America*. New York: Doubleday.

———. 2012. "The NSA Is Building the Country's Biggest Spy Center (Watch What You Say)." *Wired* 3. Accessed January 19, 2015. http://www.wired.com/2012/03/ff_nsadatacenter.

———. 2014. "The Most Wanted Man in the World." *Wired* 1. Accessed January 19, 2015. http://www.wired.com/2014/08/edward-snowden.

Barabási, Albert-László, and Eric Bonabeau. 2003. "Scale-Free Networks." *Scientific American* 5: 50–59.

Baran, Paul. 1964a. *On Distributed Communications II: Digital Simulation of Hot-Potato Routing in a Broadband Distributed Communications Network*. Santa Monica: RAND Corporation.

———. 1964b. *On Distributed Communications XI: Summary Overview*. Santa Monica: RAND Corporation.

———. 1964c. *On Distributed Communications V: History, Alternative Approaches, and Comparisons*. Santa Monica: RAND Corporation.

———. 1964d. "On Distributed Communications Networks." *IEEE Transactions* CS-12 (1): 1–9.

———. 2002. "The Beginnings of Packet Switching: Some Underlying Concepts." *IEEE Communications Magazine* 40 (7): 42–48.

Barlow, John P. 1996. "A Declaration of the Independence of Cyberspace." Accessed January 19, 2015. http://projects.eff.org/~barlow/Declaration-Final.html.

Bärwolff, Matthias. 2009. "DPI Considered Not Harmful." Accessed January 19, 2015. http://works.bepress.com/mbaer/3/.

Bar-Yanai, Roni, Michael Langberg, David Peleg, and Liam Roditty. 2010. "Realtime Classification for Encrypted Traffic." *Lecture Notes in Computer Science* 6049: 373–85.

Bauman, Zygmunt, Didier Bigo, Paulo Esteves, Elspeth Guild, Vivienne Jabri, David Lyon, and R. B. J. Walker. 2014. "After Snowden: Rethinking the Impact of Surveillance." *International Political Sociology* 8: 121–44.

118   Baxmann, Inge, Timon Beyes, and Claus Pias, eds. 2015 *Social Media and the New Masses.* Chicago: University of Chicago Press.

Beckedahl, Markus. 2009. "Netzpolitik-Podcast 081: Netzneutralität und Netzwerkmanagement." Accessed January 19, 2015. http://netzpolitik.org/2009/netzpolitik-podcast-081-netzneutralitaet-und-netzwerkmanagement.

Beckedahl, Markus, and André Meister, eds. 2014. Überwachtes Netz: Edward Snowden und der größte Überwachungsskandal der Geschichte. Berlin: Newthinking Communications.

Bedner, Mark. 2009. "Rechtmäßigkeit der 'Deep Packet Inspection'." Accessed January 19, 2015. https://kobra.bibliothek.uni-kassel.de/bitstream/urn:nbn:de:he bis:34-2009113031192/5/BednerDeepPacketInspection.pdf.

Bendrath, Ralf, and Milton Mueller. 2010. "The End of the Net as We Know It? Deep Packet Inspection and Internet Governance." Accessed January 19, 2015. http://papers.ssrn.com/sol3/papers.cfm?abstract_id=1653259.

Beniger, James R. 1986. *The Control Revolution: Technological and Economic Origins of the Information Society.* Cambridge, MA: Harvard University Press.

Bertschek, Irene, Yoo, Christopher S., Fabienne R. Rasel, and Florian Smuda. 2013. "Die Netzneutralitätsdebatte im internationalen Vergleich." Bundesministerium für Wirtschaft und Technologie. Accessed January 19, 2015. http://www.bmwi.de/BMWi/Redaktion/PDF/Publikationen/Studien/netzneutralitaetsdebatte-im-internationalen-vergleich,property=pdf,bereich=bmwi2012,sprache=de,rwb=true.pdf.

Beyes, Timon, and Claus Pias. 2014. "Transparenz und Geheimnis." *Zeitschrift für Kulturwissenschaften* 2: 111–17.

Blumenberg, Hans. 2012. *Quellen, Ströme, Eisberge.* Berlin: Suhrkamp.

Blumenthal, Marjory, and David Clark. 2001. "Rethinking the Design of the Internet: The End-to-End Arguments vs. the Brave New World." *ACM Transactions on Internet Technology* 1 (1): 70–109.

Brand, Stewart. 2003. "Founding Father." *Wired* 9 (3): 145–53.

Bunz, Mercedes. 2009. *Vom Speicher zum Verteiler: Die Geschichte des Internet.* Berlin: Kadmos.

Canguilhem, Georges. 2006. "Die Position der Epistemologie muss in der Nachhut angesiedelt sein: Ein Interview." In *Wissenschaft, Technik, Leben,* edited by Henning Schmidgen, 103–22. Berlin: Merve.

Carpenter, Brian. 1996. "Architectural Principles of the Internet: RFC 1958." Accessed January 19, 2015. https://www.ietf.org/rfc/rfc1958.txt.

Castells, Manuel. 1998. *The Information Age: Economy, Society, and Culture: End of Millennium.* Malden: Blackwell.

Cerf, Vinton, and Robert Kahn. 1974. "A Protocol for Packet Network Intercommunication." *IEEE Transactions on Communications* 22 (5): 637–48.

Chamayou, Gregoire. 2015. "A brief philosophical history of the NSA." *Radical Philosophy* 191: 2-13.

Chang, Briankle. 1996. *Deconstructing Communication.* Minneapolis: University of Minnesota Press.

Chaos Computer Club. 2010. "Forderungen für ein lebenswertes Netz."
Accessed January 19, 2015. http://www.ccc.de/en/updates/2010/
forderungen-lebenswertes-netz.

Chun, Wendy. 2011. "Crisis, Crisis, Crisis, or Sovereignty and Networks." *Theory Culture & Society* 28 (6): 91-112.

Cisco Systems. 2015. "Cisco Service Control Engine 10000 Data Sheet." Accessed January 19, 2015. http://www.cisco.com/c/en/us/products/collateral/service-exchange/sce-10000-series-service-control-engines/datasheet-c78-732339.html.

Clarke, Richard A., Michael J. Morell, Geoffrey R. Stone, Cass R. Sunstein, and Peter P. Swire. 2014. *The NSA Report: Liberty and Security in a Changing World.* Princeton: Princeton University Press.

Cohn, Cindy. 2014. "EFF Response to FBI Director Comey's Speech on Encryption." Accessed January 19, 2015. https://www.eff.org/deeplinks/2014/10/eff-response-fbi-director-comeys-speech-encryption.

Cohn, Marjorie. 2014. "Police State America: Will the US Supreme Court Apply Cell Phone Privacy to NSA Metadata Collection?" Accessed January 19, 2015. http://www.globalresearch.ca/police-state-america-will-the-us-supreme-court-apply-cell-phone-privacy-to-nsa-metadata-collection/5389211.

Comey, James. 2014. "Going Dark: Are Technology, Privacy, and Public Safety on a Collision Course?" Accessed January 19, 2015. http://www.fbi.gov/news/speeches/going-dark-are-technology-privacy-and-public-safety-on-a-collision-course.

Davies, Donald W. 2001. "An Historical Study of the Beginnings of Packet Switching." *The Computer Journal* 44 (3): 152–62.

Day, John D. 2010. *Patterns in Network Architecture: A Return to Fundamentals.* London: Pearson Education.

DeNardis, Laura. 2014. *Protocol Politics: The Globalization of Internet Governance.* Cambridge, MA: MIT Press.

Derrida, Jacques. 2001. "Structure, Sign, and Play in the Discourse of the Human Sciences." In *Writing and Difference*, translated by Alan Bass, 351–70. London: Routledge.

———. 2011. *Voice and Phenomenon: Introduction to the Problem of the Sign in Husserl's Phenomenology*, translated by Leonard Lawlor. Evanston: Northwestern University Press.

Deutsche Telekom. 2010. "Was bedeutet eigentlich Netzneutralität?" Accessed January 19, 2015. http://www.schonleben.de/wp-content/uploads/2010/09/telekom-was-bedeutet-eigentlich-netzneutralitaet.pdf.

Deutscher Bundestag. 2012. "Vierter Zwischenbericht der Enquete-Kommission *Internet und digitale Gesellschaft*: Bundestags-Drucksache Drucksache 17/8536." Accessed January 19, 2015. http://dipbt.bundestag.de/dip21/btd/17/085/1708536.pdf.

Diffie, Whitfield, and Susan E. Landau. 2010. *Privacy on the Line: The Politics of Wiretapping and Encryption.* Cambridge, MA: MIT Press.

Doppelmayr, Johann Gabriel. 1744. *Neu-entdeckte Phaemomena von bewundernswürdigen Würckungen der Natur.* Nuremburg: Fleischmann.

Electronic Frontier Foundation. 2013. "Wapo Prism Document." Accessed January 19, 2015. https://www.eff.org/document/2013-06-06-wapo-prism.

Engell, Lorenz, and Joseph Vogl. 1999. "Vorwort." In *Kursbuch Medienkultur: Die maßgeblichen Theorien von Brecht bis Baudrillard*, edited by Claus Pias et al., 8–11. Stuttgart: DVA.

Engemann, Christoph. 2010. "Verteiltes Überleben: Paul Barans Antwort auf die atomare Bedrohung." In *Überleben: Ein kulturtheoretischer Begriff*, edited by Falko Schmiederer, 381–94. Munich: Fink.

———. 2015. „Die Adresse des freien Bürgers: Digitale Identitätssysteme Deutschlands und der USA im Vergleich." *Leviathan: Berliner Zeitschrift für Sozialwissenschaft* 43 (1): 43-63.

Ernst, Wolfgang. 2007. "Zeit und Code." In *Die Szene der Gewalt: Bilder, Codes und Materialitäten*, edited by Daniel Tyradellis and Burkhardt Wolf, 175–87. Frankfurt am Main: Peter Lang.

Felten, Edward W. 2013. "Declaration of Professor Edward W. Felten." Accessed January 19, 2015. https://www.aclu.org/files/pdfs/natsec/clapper/2013.08.26%20-ACLU%20PI%20Brief%20-%20Declaration%20-%20Felten.pdf.

Foucault, Michel. 1997. "What is Critique?" In *The Politics of Truth*, translated by Lysa Hochroth, 41–81. New York: Semiotext(e).

Fung, Brian. 2014. "World Wide Web Inventor Slams Internet Fast Lanes: 'It's bribery'." Accessed January 19, 2015. http://www.washingtonpost.com/blogs/the-switch/wp/2014/09/19/world-wide-web-inventor-lashes-out-at-internet-fast-lanes-its-bribery.

Galison, Peter. 2001. "War against the Center." *Grey Room* 4 (4): 5–33.

———. 2003. *Einstein's Clocks, Poincaré's Maps: Empires of Time.* New York: Norton.

Galloway, Alexander R. 2004. *Protocol: How Control Exists after Decentralization.* Cambridge, MA: MIT Press.

Galloway, Alexander R., and Eugene Thacker. 2007. *The Exploit: A Theory of Networks.* Minneapolis: University of Minnesota Press.

Gaycken, Sandro. 2013. "Snowden opferte sein Leben für ein offenes Geheimnis." *Cicero*, 7 (8).

Gellman, Barton, and Askhan Soltani. 2013. "NSA Tracking Cellphone Locations Worldwide, Snowden Documents Show." Accessed January 19, 2015. http://www.washingtonpost.com/world/national-security/nsa-tracking-cellphone-locations-worldwide-snowden-documents-show/2013/12/04/5492873a-5cf2-11e3-bc56-c6ca94801fac_story.html.

Gießmann, Sebastian. 2009. "Netzwerk-Zeit, Zeit der Netzwerke: Fragmente zur Datenökonomie um 1960." In *Zeitkritische Medien*, edited by Axel Volmar, 239–54. Berlin: Kadmos.

———. 2014. *Die Verbundenheit der Dinge: Eine Kulturgeschichte der Netze und Netzwerke.* Kaleidogramme. Berlin: Kadmos.

———. 2015. "Im Parlament der möglichen Medienpraktiken: Anmerkungen zur Netzneutralitätskontroverse." *Mediale Kontrolle unter Beobachtung.* Forthcoming.

Gilder, George F. 2000. *Telecosm: How Infinite Bandwidth Will Revolutionize Our World.* New York: Free Press.

Gillespie, Tarleton. 2006. "Engineering a Principle: 'End-to-End' in the Design of the Internet." *Social Studies of Science* 36: 427–57.

Gorman, Siobhan, and Jennifer Valentino-DeVries. 2013. "New Details Show Broader NSA Surveillance Reach." Accessed January 19, 2015. http://online.wsj.com/articles/SB10001424127887324108204579022874091732470.

Gray, Stephen. 1731. "A Letter to Cromwell Mortimer, M. D. Secr. R. S. Containing several Experiments Concerning Electricity." *Philosophical Transactions* 37: 18–44.

Greenwald, Glenn. 2014. *No Place to Hide: Edward Snowden, the NSA and the Surveillance State.* London: Penguin.

Greenwald, Glenn, Ewen MacAskill, and Laura Poitras. 2013. "Edward Snowden: The Whistleblower behind the NSA Surveillance Revelations." Accessed January 19, 2015. http://www.theguardian.com/world/2013/jun/09/edward-snowden-nsa-whistleblower-surveillance.

Guardian. 2013. "Verizon Forced to Hand over Telephone Data – Full Court Ruling." Accessed January 19, 2015. http://www.theguardian.com/world/interactive/2013/jun/06/verizon-telephone-data-court-order.

Halpin, Harry. 2013. "Immaterial Civil War: The World Wide War on the Web." *Culture Machine* 14: 1–26.

Helmholtz, Hermann von. 1853. "On the Methods of Measuring Very Small Portions of Time, and Their Application to Physiological Purposes." *The London, Edinburgh and Dublin Philosophical Magazine and Journal of Science* In *Gesammelte Schriften* 6 (Fourth Series): 313–25.

Hesse, Mary B. 1961. *Forces and Fields: The Concept of Action at a Distance in the History of Physics.* London: Nelson.

Hill, Kashmir. 2013. "Blueprints of NSA's Ridiculously Expensive Data Center in Utah Suggest It Holds Less Info Than Thought." Accessed January 19, 2015. http://www.forbes.com/sites/kashmirhill/2013/07/24/blueprints-of-nsa-data-center-in-utah-suggest-its-storage-capacity-is-less-impressive-than-thought/.

Hörl, Erich. 2011. "Die technologische Bedingung: Zur Einführung." In *Die technologische Bedingung: Beiträge zur Beschreibung der technischen Welt*, edited by Erich Hörl, 7–53. Frankfurt am Main: Suhrkamp.

Hughes, Thomas P. 1993. *Networks of Power.* London: The Johns Hopkins University Press.

Human Rights Council. 2014. "The Right to Privacy in the Digital Age: Report of the Office of the United Nations High Commissioner for Human Rights." Accessed January 19, 2015. http://www.ohchr.org/en/hrbodies/hrc/regularsessions/session27/documents/a.hrc.27.37_en.pdf.

Human Rights Watch. 2014. "Turkey: Internet Freedom, Rights in Sharp Decline." Accessed January 19, 2015. http://www.hrw.org/news/2014/09/02/turkey-internet-freedom-rights-sharp-decline.

Ingham, Kenneth, and Stephanie Forrest. 2002. "A History and Survey of Network Firewalls." Accessed January 19, 2015. http://www.cs.unm.edu/ treport/tr/02-12/firewall.pdf.

Inkster, Nigel. 2014. "The Snowden Revelations: Myths and Misapprehensions." *Survival* 56 (1): 51–60.

122 International Telecommunication Union. 2012. "Requirements for Deep Packet Inspection in Next Generation Networks." Accessed January 19, 2015. http://www.itu.int/rec/T-REC-Y.2770-201211-I.

Jäger, Ludwig. 2004. "Störung und Transparenz: Skizze zur performativen Logik des Medialen." In *Performativität und Medialität*, edited by Sybille Krämer, 35–74. Munich: Fink.

Kammerer, Dietmar. 2015. "Software, die zur Waffe wird." *Edition Le Monde Diplomatique* 16: 38–41.

Kapp, Ernst. 1877. *Grundlinien einer Philosophie der Technik*. Braunschweig: Westermann.

Kassung, Christian, and Thomas Macho, eds. 2012. *Kulturtechniken der Synchronisation*. Munich: Fink.

Kelty, Chris. 2014a. "Against Networks." *Spheres* 1. Accessed February 16, 2015. http://cdc.leuphana.com/uploads/tx_dwwebjournal/spheres-1_kelty1.pdf

———. 2014b. "The Fog of Freedom." In *Media Technologies: Essays on Communication, Materiality, and Society*, edited by Tarleton Gillespie, Pablo J. Boczkowski, and Kirsten A. Foot, 195–220. Cambridge, MA: MIT Press.

Kirschenbaum, Matthew G. 2008. *Mechanisms: New Media and the Forensic Imagination*. Cambridge, MA: MIT Press.

Kittler, Friedrich A. 1986. "No Such Agency." *TAZ* (October 11). Quoted here from "No Such Agency," translated by Paul Feigelfeld. *Theory, Culture & Society* (February 12, 2014). Accessed February 16, 2015. http://theoryculturesociety.org/kittler-on-the-nsa/.

Kleinrock, Leonard. 1964. *Communication Nets: Stochastic Message Flow and Delay*. New York: McGraw-Hill.

Konitzer, Werner. 2005. "Telefonieren als besondere Form gedehnter Äußerung." In *Ortsgespräche: Raum und Kommunikation 19 und 20 Jahrhundert*, edited by Alexander C. Geppert, Uffa Jensen, and Jörn Weinhold, 179–99. Bielefeld: Transcript.

Krämer, Jan, Lukas Wiewiorra, and Christof Weinhardt. 2013. "Net Neutrality: A Progress Report." *Telecommunications Policy* 37 (9): 794–813.

Krämer, Sybille. 2003. "Erfüllen Medien eine Konstitutionsleistung? Thesen über die Rolle medientheoretischer Erwägungen beim Philosophieren." In *Medienphilosophie: Beiträge zur Klärung eines Begriffs*, edited by Stefan Münker, Alexander Roesler, and Mike Sandbothe, 78–90. Frankfurt am Main: Fischer.

Królikowski, Agata. 2014. "Packet Inspection in Zeiten von Big Data." In *Überwachung und Recht: Tagungsband zur Telemedicus Sommerkonferenz 2014*, edited by Telemedicus e.V., 143–64. Berlin: epubli.

Kurz, Constanze. 2011. "Das Blinzeln des Adlers." Accessed January 19, 2015. http://www.faz.net/aktuell/feuilleton/aus-dem-maschinenraum/kriegstechnik-das-blinzeln-des-adlers-11374424.html.

Landau, Susan. 2013. "Making Sense of Snowden: What's Significant in the NSA Surveillance Revelations." *IEEE Security and Privacy* 11 (4): 54–63.

———. 2014. "Making Sense of Snowden, Part II: What's Significant in the NSA Surveillance Revelations." *IEEE Security and Privacy* 12 (1): 66–75.

Lemke, Martin. 2008. "Die Praxis polizeilicher Überwachung: Geschichten aus dem Alltag." In *1984.exe: Gesellschaftliche, politische und juristische Aspekte moderner Überwachungstechnologien*, edited by Sandro Gaycken and Constanze Kurz, 167–79. Bielefeld: Transcript.

Lessig, Lawrence. 2004. *Free Culture: How Big Media Uses Technology and the Law to Lock Down Culture and Control Creativity.* New York: Penguin.

Lobo, Sascha. 2014. "Die digitale Kränkung des Menschen." Accessed January 19, 2015. http://www.faz.net/aktuell/feuilleton/debatten/abschied-von-der-utopie-die-digitale-kraenkung-des-menschen-12747258.html.

Loebel, Jens-Martin. 2011. "Aus dem Tagebuch eines Selbstaufzeichners: Interview geführt von Ute Holl und Claus Pias." *Zeitschrift für Medienwissenschaft* 4: 115–26.

Loewenstein, Anthony. 2014. "The Ultimate Goal of the NSA is Total Population Control." Accessed January 19, 2015. http://www.theguardian.com/commentisfree/2014/jul/11/the-ultimate-goal-of-the-nsa-is-total-population-control.

Lovink, Geert. 2014. "Hermes on the Hudson: Notes on Media Theory after Snowden." *eflux* 54 (4). Accessed January 19, 2015. http://www.e-flux.com/journal/hermes-on-the-hudson-notes-on-media-theory-after-snowden/.

Lyon, David. 2014. "Surveillance, Snowden, and Big Data: Capacities, Consequences, Critique." *Big Data & Society* 1 (2): 1–13.

March, James G., and Johan P. Olsen. 1976. *Ambiguity and Choice in Organizations.* Bergen: Universitetsforlaget.

Marsden, Christopher T. 2010. *Net Neutrality: Towards a Co-Regulatory Solution.* London: Bloomsbury.

Martini, Mario. 2011. "Wie viel Gleichheit braucht das Internet? Netzneutralität zwischen kommunikativer Chancengleichheit und Infrastruktureffizienz." *Speyerer Vorträge* 96. Accessed January 19, 2015. http://www.dhv-speyer.de/PUBL/Vortraege/Heft96.pdf.

McKelvey, Fenwick. 2010. "Ends and Ways: The Algorithmic Politics of Network Neutrality." *Global Media Journal* 3 (1): 51–73.

McLuhan, Marshall. 1964. *Understanding Media: The Extensions of Man.* New York: Mentor.

McLuhan, Marshall, and Barrington Nevitt. 1973. "The Argument: Causality in the Electric World." *Technology and Culture* 14 (1): 1–18.

Merkel, Angela. 2014. "Rede von Bundeskanzlerin Merkel zum *Digitising Europe Summit* am 4. Dezember 2014." Accessed January 19, 2015. http://www.bundes-regierung.de/Content/DE/Rede/2014/12/2014-12-04-merkel-digitising-europe-summit.html.

Mersch, Dieter. 2004. "Medialität und Undarstellbarkeit: Einleitung in eine 'negative' Medientheorie." In *Performativität und Medialität*, edited by Sybille Krämer, 75–96. Munich: Fink.

Mestmacher-Steiner, Christoph. 2014. "Interview with Edward Snowden." Accessed January 19, 2015. https://www.tagesschau.de/snowden-interview-englisch100.pdf.

124   Mueller, Milton. 2004. *Ruling the Root: Internet Governance and the Taming of Cyber-space.* Cambridge, MA: MIT Press.

National Security Agency. 2013. "Missions, Authorities, Oversight and Partnerships." Accessed January 19, 2015. https://www.nsa.gov/public_info/_files/speeches_testimonies/2013_08_09_the_nsa_story.pdf

Nunes, Rodrigo. 2014. *Organisation of the Organisationless: Collective Action after Networks.* Lüneburg: Mute.

Parikka, Jussi. 2012. *What is Media Archaeology?* Cambridge, UK: Polity Press.

Paßmann, Johannes. 2014. "Baumhaus und Hausrecht: Netzneutralität zwischen historischem Ideal und technisch-ökonomischer Wirklichkeit." In *Wir nennen es Wirklichkeit: Denkanstöße zur Netzkultur*, edited by Peter Kemper, Alf Mentzer, and Julika Tillmanns, 235–53. Leipzig: Reclam.

Peters, John D. 2000. *Speaking into the Air: A History of the Idea of Communication.* Chicago: University of Chicago Press.

Pias, Claus. 2009. "Time of Non-Reality: Miszellen zum Thema Zeit und Auflösung." In *Zeitkritische Medien*, edited by Axel Volmar, 267–81. Berlin: Kadmos.

Plate, Jürgen. 2004. "Grundlagen Computernetze." Accessed January 19, 2015. http://www.netzmafia.de/skripten/netze/index.html.

Rensselaer, Cortlandt van. 1858. *Signals from the Atlantic Cable: An Address Delivered at the Telegraphic Celebration.* Philadelphia: Wilson.

Rieger, Frank. 2008. "Abhören und Lokalisieren von Telefonen: Der Stand der Dinge." In *1984.exe: Gesellschaftliche, politische und juristische Aspekte moderner Überwachungstechnologien*, edited by Sandro Gaycken and Constanze Kurz, 53–66. Bielefeld: Transcript.

Riley, Chris M., and Ben Scott. 2009. "Deep Packet Inspection: The End of the Internet as We Know It?" Accessed January 19, 2015. http://www.freepress.net/files/Deep_Packet_Inspection_The_End_of_the_Internet_As_We_Know_It.pdf.

Rohrhuber, Julian. 2009. "Das Rechtzeitige: Doppelte Extension und formales Experiment." In *Zeitkritische Medien*, edited by Axel Volmar, 195–212. Berlin: Kadmos.

Saar, Martin. 2008. "Genealogische Kritik." In *Was ist Kritik? Philosophische Positionen*, edited by Rahel Jaeggi and Tilo Wesche, 247–65. Frankfurt am Main: Suhrkamp.

Saltzer, J. H, D. P Reed, and D. D Clark. 1984. "End-to-End-Arguments in System Design." *ACM Transactions on Computer Systems* 2 (4): 277–88.

Sandvig, Christian. 2007. "Network Neutrality is the New Common Carriage." *info* 9 (2/3): 136–47.

Savage, Charlie. 2013. "U.S. Weighs Wide Overhaul of Wiretap Laws." Accessed January 19, 2015. http://www.nytimes.com/2013/05/08/us/politics/obama-may-back-fbi-plan-to-wiretap-web-users.html.

Scheuerman, William E. 2014. "Whistleblowing as Civil Disobedience: The Case of Edward Snowden." *Philosophy Social Criticism* 40 (7): 609–28.

Schröter, Jens. 2004. *Das Netz und die Virtuelle Realität: Zur Selbstprogrammierung der Gesellschaft durch die universelle Maschine.* Bielefeld: Transcript.

Scola, Nancy. 2014. "Obama's Gone 'Old-School Net Neutrality': A Tim Wu Q&A." Accessed January 19, 2015. http://www.washingtonpost.com/blogs/the-switch/wp/2014/11/10/obamas-gone-old-school-net-neutrality-a-tim-wu-qa/.

Schewick, Barbara van. 2010. *Internet Architecture and Innovation*. Cambridge, MA: MIT Press.

Seemann, Michael. 2015. *Digital Tailspin. 10 Rules for the Internet after Snowden*. Amsterdam: Institute of Network Cultures. Accessed January 19, 2015. http://networkcultures.org/wp-content/uploads/2015/03/NN09_Digital_Tailspin_SP.pdf

Serres, Michel. 1982. *The Parasite*, translated by Lawrence R. Schehr. Baltimore: The Johns Hopkins University Press.

Siegert, Bernhard. 1999. *Relays: Literature as an Epoch of the Postal System*, translated by Kevin Repp. Stanford: Stanford University Press.

Siemens, Werner. 1866. "Die electrische Telegraphie." In *Sammlung gemeinverständlicher wissenschaftlicher Vorträge*, edited by Rudolf Virchow and Friedrich von Holtzendorff, 1–40. Berlin: Lüderitz'sche Verlagsbuchhandlung.

Siering, Peter. 2011. "28C3: Hacker kämpfen für 'echtes Netz' und 'echte Computer'." Accessed January 19, 2015. http://www.heise.de/newsticker/meldung/28C3-Hacker-kaempfen-fuer-echtes-Netz-und-echte-Computer-1401796.html.

Sietmann, Richard. 2011. "Schmalspur: Der Kampf gegen die Netzneutralität zielt auf die Vereinnahmung des Internet." *c't Magazin für Computertechnik* 8: 158–65.

Singel, Ryan. 2007. "Point, Click … Eavesdrop: How the FBI Wiretap Net Operates." Accessed January 19, 2015. http://www.wired.com/politics/security/news/2007/08/wiretap?

Sonne, Paul, and David Gauthier-Villars. 2012. "Tech Firm Amesys Faces French Judicial Probe." Accessed January 19, 2015. http://www.wsj.com/articles/SB10001424052702304791704577420392081640000.

Sprenger, Florian. 2012. *Medien des Immediaten: Elektrizität, Telegraphie, McLuhan*. Berlin: Kadmos.

Steinmetz, Kevin F. 2012. "WikiLeaks and Realpolitik." *Journal of Theoretical and Philosophical Criminology* 4 (1): 14–52.

Sutherland, Thomas. 2012. "Liquid Networks and the Metaphysics of Flux: Ontologies of Flow in an Age of Speed and Mobility." *Theory, Culture & Society* 30 (5): 3–23.

Taureck, Bernhard H. F. 2014. Überwachungsdemokratie: Die NSA als Religion. Munich: Fink.

Thacker, Eugene. 2004. "Networks, Swarms, Multitudes." *Ctheory* 18. Accessed January 19, 2015. http://www.ctheory.net/articles.aspx?id=422.

US Congress. 1996. "Communications Assistance for Law Enforcement Act, August 19, 1996." Accessed January 19, 2015. http://legcounsel.house.gov/Comps/Communications%20Assistance%20For%20Law%20Enforcement%20Act.pdf.

United Nations. 1948. "The Universal Declaration of Human Rights." Accessed March 1, 2015. http://www.un.org/en/documents/udhr/.

Used Cisco Info. Accessed January 19, 2015. http://www.usedcisco.info/CISCO.

Virilio, Paul. 2000. *Polar Inertia*, translated by Patrick Camiller. London: SAGE, 2000.

Warnke, Martin. 2014. " Databases as citadels in the web 2.0." In *Unlike Us Reader: Social Media Monopolies and the Their Alternatives*, edited by Geert Lovink and Miriam Rasch, 76-89, Inge Baxmann, Timon Beyes, and Claus Pias, 135–50. Amsterdam: Institute of Network Cultures.

Weis, Rüdiger. 2012. "Nacktscanner fürs Internet." *TAZ* (September 24, 2012). Accessed January 19, 2015. http://www.taz.de/!102271/.

Wheatstone, Charles. 1834. "An Account of Some Experiments to Measure the Velocity of Electricity and the Duration of Electric Light." *Philosophical Transactions* 124: 583–91.

White House. 2013. "Press Conference by the President." Accessed January 19, 2015. http://www.whitehouse.gov/the-press-office/2013/12/20/press-conference-president.

———. 2014. "Statement by the President on Net Neutrality." Accessed January 19, 2015. http://www.whitehouse.gov/the-press-office/2014/11/10/statement-president-net-neutrality.

Whitney, Lance. 2010. "Tim Berners-Lee: The Web is Threatened." Accessed January 19, 2015. http://www.cnet.com/news/tim-berners-lee-the-web-is-threatened/.

WikiLeaks. 2011. "The Spy Files." Accessed January 19, 2015. http://wikileaks.org/spyfiles.

Worldwide Human Rights Movement. 2013. "Amesys Case: The Investigation Chamber Green Lights the Investigative Proceedings on the Sale of Surveillance Equipment by Amesys to the Khadafi Regime." Accessed January 19, 2015. http://www.fidh.org/en/north-africa-middle-east/libya/Amesys-Case-The-Investigation-12752.

Wu, Tim. 2003. "Network Neutrality, Broadband Discrimination." *Journal of Telecommunications and High Technology Law* 3: 141–76.

———. 2009. "Tim Wu on Packet Inspection." Accessed January 19, 2015. https://www.youtube.com/watch?v=YKwgc_HQhMs.

———. 2015. "Network Neutrality FAQ." Accessed January 19, 2015. http://timwu.org/network_neutrality.html.

About the Author

Florian Sprenger is PostDoc at the *Digital Cultures Research Lab* at Leuphana Universität Lüneburg. He works on the media history of electricity, the transition of environments into technical surroundings, the history of the future, infrastructures of architecture and theories of media. Among his publications are *Medien des Immediaten – Elektrizität, Telegraphie, McLuhan* (2012), *Die Enden des Kabels* (mit Daniel Gethmann, 2014), *Blitzlicht* (mit Katja Müller-Helle, 2012) and articles covering topics such as standards, environments, immediacies and jumps.